THE MOST
IMPORTANT ACT

The Most Important Act

Ebenezer Agboola
Emmanuel Adewusi

The Agboola Ministries

Contents

Dedication	vii
Acknowledgments	ix
Introduction	xi
1 The Indispensable Act	1
2 Reasons for the Act	26
3 Types and Methods	45
4 The Hurdle and How to Overcome	61
5 Conclusion	83
Contact the Author	87
About the Book	89
About the Author	91

The Most Important Act
Copyright © 2020 by Ebenezer Agboola

All rights reserved. No part of this book may be reproduced in any manner whatsoever without written permission except in the case of brief quotations Embodied in critical articles and reviews.

First Printing, 2020

Scripture quotations are taken from the Holy Bible, New Living Translation, copyright ©1996, 2004, 2007, 2013, 2015 by Tyndale House Foundation. Used by permission of Tyndale House Publishers, Inc., Carol Stream, Illinois 60188. All rights reserved.

Scripture quotes marked (KJV) are taken from the King James Version of the Bible. Scripture quotes marked (NKJV) are taken from the New King James Version, Copyright © 1982 Thomas Nelson. All rights reserved.

Any people depicted in stock imagery provided by Thinkstock are models and such images are being used for illustrative purposes only.

ISBN: 978-1-7775029-4-2 (sc)
ISBN: 978-1-7775029-5-9 (e)

Cover Design by Shimona DaCosta.

Dedication

To my Father in Heaven, the master planner. You are the reason for everything. You made all things beautiful (including this book) in its own time (**Ecclesiastes 3:11).** You planned it and you brought it to fruition. Thank you for choosing me as a vessel and for being an awesome Father.

To the lover of my soul; my savior and Lord—Jesus, the door to all good things (**John 10:9**). If not for Your sacrifice on the cross, none of these (including this book) will be possible. I am eternally grateful for the access You gave through the cross those years ago.

To my indispensable companion and helper—the Holy Spirit, You are the one with the light of the Word. You basically authored this book. I am eternally grateful for Your patience and love. Thank You for always being there for everything (including this book) and for choosing me as a vessel.

To the members of Cornerstone Christian Church of God Edmonton. The revelation of this book came when I had the opportunity to teach in one of the services. Thank you for the impact you made on my life, my family and my ministry.

To all my fellow believers all around the world, this is a message from our Father to you.

Acknowledgments

In **Genesis 1:28 NLT**, the Lord told Adam to *fill the earth and govern it.* Therefore, you and I, as believers are destined to govern the earth. We are the head and not the tail says the lord in **Deuteronomy 28:13**. This simply means that the earth is our domain. For God or the devil to do anything here on earth, a human vessel is needed. Therefore, every plan of God requires the call. So, the call of God is to fulfil His plan here on earth.

When God calls, He does this according to His own capacity not that of the one He called. Therefore, every call of God is very capable of being extremely great. In this way, we see that throughout history God has called the least possible candidate. Someone said, God, qualifies the call and not the other way around. It is therefore wise to depend on the caller when we receive God's call. Because without Him it is simply impossible to attain the height he has destined.

Due to the enormousness of God's call, every call has people appointed to help in fulfilling that call. Yes, I am called a teacher, and as such with the help of the Holy Spirit, I have written this book. However, this is not the end but rather the beginning of the finished product you are reading now. Having content to write does not equal a great book, but having God ordained people for the right purposes does. Therefore, I would like to acknowledge each and every vessel used by God in bringing His vision to fruition.

Joanna Shandro, I am grateful for your skills. Your profession is definitely a plus. You went through the manuscript at the very first stage, or shall I call it the rough stage. With diligence and thoroughness, you brought a whole different perspective to things and for that I am grateful.

Mariam Tientchu, your editing skills, professionalism and candor when it comes to things of value is something, I am deeply grateful to God for. Thank you for being a helping hand, I am grateful.

Pastor Emmanuel Adewusi, I am grateful to God for having a spiritual father like you. Thank you for your massive contribution to this book. One of the qualifications of a father is to always be there for their children. From figuring out who I am in God, to knowing my calling and walking in it, you have been an extension of Jehovah Shammah. A vessel of God's help all through. I am eternally grateful for the zeal to see everyone around you attain their God-ordained purpose.

Shimona DaCosta. I am grateful to God for giving you such an amazing design skill. God bless you.

Introduction

As Christians, there are certain actions and reactions that define us. These I call, "the Christian ways of life." These ways are given to us mainly through the Word of God. Some of these actions and reactions are prayer, faith, love, holiness, evangelism, baptism, praise and many more. In this book, we will focus on one of them.

It is important to note that these ways are set in place because of the merciful nature of God. His dictates come with blessings if done as He has described (See **Deuteronomy 30:10-11**).

It is unfortunately sad that many children of God today are ignorant of these things. Some only know a portion, and others just simply do not understand them.

For these types of Christians, their lack of knowledge and/or understanding restricts them from certain blessings. This is so because they are not fulfilling these blessings' prerequisites. Actions and reactions are birthed out of understanding. Once we know these ways of life (acquire knowledge), it is our understanding that will dictate the necessary prerequisites (right actions) needed for the blessing. Hence, the need for understanding. However, it is impossible to understand without knowledge.

The Necessity of Knowledge

> *My people are destroyed for lack of knowledge. (**Hosea 4:6a KJV**).*

The Bible verse above reveals to us that lack of knowledge, also known as ignorance, is a possible root of destruction. What we do not know is very capable of killing us. As Christians, we cannot afford not to know, because of the nature of the kind of battle that we fight (see **Ephesians 6:12**). Our enemy, the devil, will find it interestingly easy to claim victory when we lack knowledge. We need the right knowledge at the right time to surf through issues of life. It is important we understand that the life of a Christian is that of a person who is always learning and seeking knowledge all the days of his/her life. Hence, the need for God in every day of his/her life.

Christ's gift of hierarchy structure to the church, and Apostle Paul's command to not forsake the gathering of fellow believers, are for this reason: to acquire knowledge and understanding.

> *Now, these are the gifts Christ gave to the church: the apostles, the prophets, the evangelists, and the pastors and teachers. Their responsibility is to equip God's people to do his work and build up the church, the body of Christ. This will continue until we all come to such unity in our faith and knowledge of God's Son that we will be mature in the*

*Lord, measuring up to the full and complete standard of Christ. (**Ephesians 4:11-13 NLT**)*

*And let us not neglect our meeting together, as some people do, but encourage one another, especially now that the day of his return is drawing near. (**Hebrews 10:25 NLT**)*

The scriptures above confirm that these hierarchies in Christianity, and Paul's command, are to help us seek knowledge. The truth is, God wants us to ask questions of the people in these positions of hierarchy to help us. This is really one of the many reasons why God has placed them in these positions.

Some might say, "I hear from God directly, therefore, I don't need any human to acquire knowledge." I am happy that you hear from God, but what people don't realize is that the human mind is very fragile. And depending on how God speaks to us, our minds can interpret things differently in each situation. So, it is always a good practice to confirm what we get from God with His written word—the Bible, and another unbiased trusted source connected to God before jumping into action.

*This is the third time I am coming to visit you (and as the Scriptures say, "The facts of every case must be established by the testimony of two or three witnesses"). (**2 Corinthians 13:1 NLT**)*

Also, there are things God will tell us directly and some He will only reveal through Christ's gift of hierarchies and/or fellow believers. It is because of the possibility of God speaking through our fellow believers that Apostle Paul encouraged us to not forsake our gatherings (See **Hebrews 10:25** and **1 Thessalonians 5:11**). In many cases, the key to freedom from our current dilemma lies in another fellow believer's experience(s) and/or struggle(s). Our fellow believers may possess a key that we desperately need. Nonetheless, it is possible that this key may only be acquired through the possible pain of experience (sometimes, the time lost is pain enough). So, why go through the pain when we can get the key without the pain? In this case, other believer's experience(s) and/or struggle(s) can become a source of encouragement and freedom for us.

Some of these keys we can get in person when we talk and often, they are kept and locked up in anointed books such as the Bible. Truth is, all keys to freedom are locked up in the Bible. Nevertheless, when we read the accounts of people who lived or are living in our day and age coupled with the principles of the Bible, it puts things in a real and relatable perspective for us. Reading the Bible and anointed books such as this are very important for our growth. In Christianity, our growth is hung on reading, learning and thoroughly seeking knowledge in every God-ordained way.

Regarding the gifts of Christ to the church, some of the people in these hierarchy positions can also be deemed as our spiritual authorities. And as such God can speak certain things through them to us as well. To explain this point, let us examine the life of Moses, the great prophet.

When Moses married an Ethiopian woman, his siblings rightfully disagreed with him. But the Lord testified on behalf of Moses to his siblings (Miriam and Aaron). He mentioned the fact that He speaks to Moses face-to-face, unlike other prophets. Yet it took Moses' father-in-law, Jethro, who was a priest (a form of hierarchy position and spiritual authority) in Midian to advise Moses on ways to structure things in a way not so harmful to his health? Below is the account from the scriptures.

> *And the LORD said to them, Now, listen to what I say: "If there were prophets among you, I, the LORD, would reveal myself in visions. I would speak to them in dreams. But not with my servant Moses. Of all my house, he is the one I trust. I speak to him face to face, clearly, and not in riddles! He sees the LORD as he is. So why were you not afraid to criticize my servant Moses?" (**Numbers 12:6-8 NLT**)*
>
> *The next day, Moses took his seat to hear the people's disputes against each other. They waited before him from morning till evening. When Moses' father-in-law saw all that Moses was doing for the people, he asked, "What are you really accomplishing here? Why are you trying to do all this alone while everyone stands around you from morning till evening?" Moses replied, "Because the people come to me to get a ruling from God. When a dispute arises, they come to me, and I am the one who settles the case between the quarreling parties. I inform the people of God's decrees and give them his instructions." "This is not good!" Moses' father-in-law exclaimed. "You're going*

> to wear yourself out—and the people, too. This job is too heavy a burden for you to handle all by yourself. Now listen to me, and let me give you a word of advice, and may God be with you. You should continue to be the people's representative before God, bringing their disputes to him. Teach them God's decrees and give them his instructions. Show them how to conduct their lives. But select from all the people some capable, honest men who fear God and hate bribes. Appoint them as leaders over groups of one thousand, one hundred, fifty, and ten. They should always be available to solve the people's common disputes but have them bring the major cases to you. Let the leaders decide the smaller matters themselves. They will help you carry the load, making the task easier for you. If you follow this advice, and if God commands you to do so, then you will be able to endure the pressures, and all these people will go home in peace." Moses listened to his father-in-law's advice and followed his suggestions. (***Exodus 18:13-24 NLT***).

Looking at this scenario, the fair question to ask is, why would God not tell Moses what Jethro advised in one of their face-to-face encounters? The Lord wants us to be submissive and humble, but to do this we must be under God's direct and His human-ordained authorities. Hence, the necessity of the gifts of Christ to the church. If God tells us everything directly, then there would be no reason to respect or even submit to any human authority; and thus pride (which is of the devil) sets in and this can lead to our downfall.

Therefore, not all knowledge will come from God directly

to us, some will come from Him through His ordained human vessels.

The Necessity of Understanding

We have discussed the necessity of knowledge and a few ways we can acquire it in Christianity. However, knowing is never enough. We cannot claim to have the knowledge of success to be successful; we must understand the information we have, and act based on this understanding to be successful. When this is done properly, it is wisdom. We can see that acquiring knowledge is in fact the first step to what is needed for action(s). Understanding is therefore essential; we can know but if we do not understand, we cannot take the right action(s), which is as if we do not know.

When we lack understanding, we are susceptible to the devil. He can even use the knowledge we have to cause harm. We are a time bomb waiting to explode; in other words, we are dangerous to ourselves and everyone around us when we have knowledge with no understanding. This is so because understanding defines the right actions. So, lack of understanding usually means either no action or wrong actions, and this will cause issues/damages for us and everyone around. Think of it like a soldier on the battlefield with a rifle, who has no idea how it operates. We can agree that he is a threat to both the enemy and his squad. With what he's got, he can easily un-deliberately kill anybody including himself. Such a soldier, without training, is the most dangerous on the battlefield and will probably be the first to die; thus, causing his family to lose a loved one and his battalion to fight with one man short.

Truth is, when we lack understanding, as Christians, we have done nothing wrong. But we are injured. In the spiritual realm, having information is never enough. In the same way, an injury can lead to death, if not properly cared for, so it is that lack of understanding can push one to sin, which leads to spiritual death (see **Romans 6:23**). Lack of understanding makes us vulnerable Christians, and with the constant battle happening with our enemy, the devil, it can easily bring such a person down. It is simple logic: we are soldiers, and no good soldier goes into a fight with any form of injury.

Endure suffering along with me, as a good soldier of Christ Jesus. (**2 Timothy 2:3 NLT**)

For we are not fighting against flesh-and-blood enemies, but against evil rulers and authorities of the unseen world, against mighty powers in this dark world, and against evil spirits in the heavenly places. (**Ephesian 6:12 NLT**)

This is why when we find ourselves in a battle with the devil, he will always challenge that weak spot of ours. For example, he may force unsure thoughts about God to get us to deny or doubt God. This is the devil's strategy to attack our injured spot.

Stay alert! Watch out for your great enemy, the devil. He prowls around like a roaring lion, looking for someone (who lacks understanding) to devour. (**1 Peter 5:8 NLT; emphasis added**)

The Bible stressed the importance of acquiring understanding for all. However, this is advice for Christians and not a command.

> *Wisdom is the principal thing; therefore, get wisdom. And in all your getting, get understanding.* (**Proverbs 4:7 NKJV**)

It is advice because unlike some other instructions/commands of the Bible, lack of *certain* spiritual understanding is not a sin. However, the lack of understanding of salvation is the highway to hell. What? Yes, this is the truth and not heresy. Many might think, since understanding is very essential to Christian living, saying lack of any kind of understanding is not a sin seems incorrect. No, it's not, and I will use Jesus' proverb in Luke's account to explain this.

> *Jesus said, "There was a certain rich man who was splendidly clothed in purple and fine linen and who lived each day in luxury. At his gate lay a poor man named Lazarus who was covered with sores. As Lazarus lay there longing for scraps from the rich man's table, the dogs would come and lick his open sores. "Finally, the poor man died and was carried by the angels to sit beside Abraham at the heavenly banquet. The rich man also died and was buried, and he went to the place of the dead. There, in torment, he saw Abraham in the far distance with Lazarus at his side."The rich man shouted, 'Father Abraham, have some pity! Send Lazarus over here to dip the tip of his finger in water and cool my tongue. I am in anguish in these flames."But Abraham said to him, 'Son, remember that*

during your lifetime you had everything you wanted, and Lazarus had nothing. So now he is here being comforted, and you are in anguish. And besides, there is a great chasm separating us. No one can cross over to you from here, and no one can cross over to us from there.' (**Luke 16:19-26 NLT**).

Let us zoom in on Lazarus here, the Bible made us understand that he died a poor man and went to heaven to rest on the bosom of Abraham. The irony here is, Lazarus was poor while here on earth, but Abraham was wealthy. This might seem counterintuitive because as a child of God who owns all things (See **Psalm 24:1**), we can say poverty should not be for Christians. But that is a choice each Christian will have to make. Do you want to be wealthy like Abraham or poor like Lazarus? David's declaration in Psalms and the Apostle Paul's prayer does in fact confirm the statement that Christians should not be poor. As Christians (children of God), we are not meant to be poor. So, why was Lazarus poor?

If I were hungry, I would not tell you, for all the world is mine and everything in it. (**Psalm 50:12 NLT**)

A psalm of David. The LORD is my shepherd; I have all that I need. (**Psalm 23:1 NLT**)

And this same God who takes care of me will supply all your needs from his glorious riches, which have been given to us in Christ Jesus. (**Philippians 4:19 NLT**)

From Luke, we can deduce that Lazarus made it to heaven. This confirms that he was a child of God. So, Lazarus understood that you must be a child of God to make heaven—the understanding of salvation. Lazarus may or may not have this knowledge of wealth, but he sure lacks the understanding of this blessing and this made him a beggar for some part of his lifetime. This is the same today; many Christians can be deemed as poor because they lack this understanding. But we can all agree that Lazarus only made it to heaven after death because he was a child of God and not a sinner. A sinner is a person who lacks the understanding of salvation message and hence does not follow the commands of God at all (See **2 Corinthians 4:4**).

> *Nothing evil will be allowed to enter, nor anyone who practices shameful idolatry and dishonesty--but only those whose names are written in the Lamb's Book of Life.* (***Revelations 21:27 NLT***)

So, this confirms the fact that a lack of certain understanding after salvation may not be a sin. But we may say well, the Bible will not give such advice if there is no danger looming. This is true, lack of certain understanding may not be a sin, but there is a danger of sin because it is an injury that can lead one to sin if not properly cared for.

Furthermore, we have only one enemy and that is the devil. His goal is to make sure that we go against God at every and any possible time. He never backs down, but he's always after us to ensure that we go against God (sin). He has only one trick rolled up in his sleeve and it is deception.

Deception is making lies, or half-true appear as though it is the truth. In other words, you have been deceived when you are influenced in any way to go against God's way.

> *But I am not surprised! Even Satan disguises himself as an angel of light. (**2 Corinthians 11:14 NLT**)*

This was what he used to bring Adam and Eve into sin in **Genesis 3**. He used this all through the scriptures. Every sin in the Bible can be connected to the deception of the devil. Though it appears as a new trick each time, this is because Satan (also known as the devil) has been doing this for a long time and he is quite good at it (just like the popular saying: practice makes perfect, right?). He has been using this on humans long before you and I were born.

Deception puts us in the bondage of the devil, where we become his puppet, but the work of Jesus on the cross has enlightened us and given us the tool required to defeat the devil, and his device. This tool is the truth that comes from acquiring knowledge and thoroughly understanding it.

> *And you will know the truth, and the truth will set you free. (**John 8:32 NLT**)*

> *So that Satan will not outsmart us. For we are familiar with his evil schemes. (**2 Corinthians 2:11 NLT**)*

From **John 8:32** above, Jesus was explaining the fact that there is no freedom without the truth. The truth illuminates and enlightens. Just as light shines through the darkness, the truth shines through lies, half-truths and deception. Therefore, absolute truth is the light; and all else is darkness which is of the devil.

All truth comes from only one source and this is God through the Holy Spirit. He is the only one who can tell or show/reveal the truth to us. In fact, His name is the Spirit of truth.

> *When the Spirit of truth comes, he will guide you into all truth. He will not speak on his own but will tell you what he has heard. He will tell you about the future.* (**John 16:13 NLT**)

And since truth brings freedom, the Spirit of truth is, therefore, the Spirit of freedom. Hence, the declaration in the scripture below.

> *For the Lord is the Spirit, and wherever the Spirit of the Lord is, there is freedom.* (**2 Corinthians 3:17 NLT**)

Nothing becomes the truth to us until we have a basic understanding of it. Sometimes, this might just mean seeing the truth at work or in existence. Though it is the truth, understanding is required to ascertain the facts. In the court of law, facts are examined to reveal, locate, find, and/or sort for the truth. This is done by lawyers and sometimes expert witnesses who are required to provide a basic understanding, as necessary. Ideally, as in the case of the court, proofs are all that is needed to generate the truth. These proofs will provide the necessary understanding of the truth. The popular expression "seeing is believing" confirms this fact. Once you see it, you have the truth about its existence. Hence **Mark 16:20** and **Hebrews 2:4**. Even though not everybody understands the mechanics behind the movement and functionality of a car, almost everyone is capable of learning how to drive. Also, we all believe that the car will move when it is engaged properly. This is because we have seen it and therefore it has become the truth to us. If the car does not function as the truth that we have believed and understood, we know something is wrong.

However, I must be very clear that though proofs help to understand in the physical, many are times in Christendom, we are required to have faith. *Faith is the confidence that what we hope for will actually happen; it gives us assurance about things we cannot see (**Hebrews 11:1 NLT**).* This is the opposite of seeing proof. Also, **2 Corinthians 5:7 NLT** states: *for, we live by believing and not by seeing.* This just simply means that we trust God to do what he has promised or we have asked Him. This is because **Ephesians 3:20 NLT** declares that Our God *is able, through his mighty power at work within us, to accomplish infinitely more than we might ask or think.* Therefore, in many cases, faith will replace proof for Christians.

We do not always have the luxury of physical proof, but we must always have faith in the infinite capacity of our God. Faith is available to us all because **Romans 10:17 NLT** states that *faith comes from hearing, that is, hearing the Good News about Christ.* Therefore, regardless of what it is physically, we must always get our understanding directly from God through His word(s) and through the help of the Holy Spirit. When understanding is acquired from the word of God, faith will follow, hence **Romans 10:17**. Putting to good use the teachers and men/women of God (the hierarchies mentioned earlier) that God has given to us, is another good way to acquire understanding.

Due to the importance of understanding, the Bible encourages us to seek understanding (See **Proverbs 4:7**). This is so that we can know the truth; once we have it, we can engage it properly to gain freedom from deception.

The goal of this book is to enlighten Christians and to present the truth to us. This is because until we know and understand what the most important act today is, from the creator's (God's) point of view, we cannot do it properly and/or effectively. Therefore, we cannot get the blessing that comes with it.

Before we continue in our journey through the pages of this book, I want you to pause here and ask God to give you His intended understanding of the information presented in this book.

1

The Indispensable Act

As we will see from this chapter, the most important act today is evangelism. It is indispensable because there is literally no substitution for it. As per google, evangelism is the act of spreading the gospel of Jesus through witnessing and/or preaching. It also states that it is zealous advocacy for a cause. Though these definitions are accurate, we will focus on God's inspired definition. For every concept of God comes with a purpose and a deeper level of understanding. So, what is God's stance on evangelism?

Stance One – The Kingdom Currency

Currency is a form of legal tender used for a transaction in a region, domain, and/or kingdom. In other words, this simply means if I need something that you have that thing in your possession and are willing to let it go for a price, I could potentially offer you the acceptable legal tender in exchange for the product. That way you get what you want which is money and/or getting rid of the product; while I get what I possibly need as well. The situation of using the currency for trading gives a solution where everyone benefits; you win, and I win.

This is the same way with evangelism. It is a metaphorical legal tender when it comes to the kingdom of God. It is the currency we spend, to get what we need or desire. God has everything we could ever need, want, or desire and He wants all souls that are in our domain to be part of His kingdom (See **1 Timothy 2:4**). So, a reasonable exchange for us will be to do all we can to give God what He wants. This exchange is therefore only possible through evangelism, and it is, therefore, the legal tender of the kingdom of God. As Christians, we are on earth physically, but spiritually we belong to and operate in the kingdom of God (See **John 17:16**). In the same way, that currency can get us what we need, want, and desires here on earth, spreading the good news about Jesus can get us what we desire spiritually in the kingdom of God. So far it is legally acquirable—that is, according to the will of God (See **1 John 5:14**).

For better understanding, suppose I offer money to a seller who has the product I want or need, he/she is happy to let go of what I want or need. The seller now has the freedom to do whatever he/she pleases with the money. The truth is, when we evangelize and get a soul into God's kingdom, God becomes joyful. This is because now, our effort(s) has given God the freedom to connect directly with and make this new soul the best He had planned and envisioned for them to be as per **Jeremiah 29:11**. This would be impossible, even for

God (See **Acts 10**), unless we get this salvation message across through evangelism.

In the same way, there is more joy in heaven over one lost sinner who repents and returns to God than over ninety-nine others who are righteous and haven't strayed away! (***Luke 15:7 NLT***)

Furthermore, most of the basic understanding of the functionality of our currency here on earth is the same for the kingdom currency, evangelism. For example, quality and quantity often come with higher prices. Therefore, the more currency you have, or the more you are willing to spend, the higher the quality and/or the more quantity you can acquire. This is synonymous with evangelism as well. This is in the sense that the more engaged we are in evangelism, the richer we are spiritually, and the more God is pleased with us. When God is pleased, He gives us access to the impossible, and our heart's desires easily manifest. Hence **Proverbs 11:30.**

Financial wealth here on earth enables people to live an abundant life. Lack of money denies us many possibilities. In most advanced countries, the government provides help to people who lack enough money. This is to help them get by. In God's kingdom, where we operate spiritually, the moment we become children of God, we are entitled to basic provisions from God. Therefore, an abundance of currency will give us the ability to purchase as much as we can afford. Abundance evangelism gives us the ability to acquire as much as we can afford in the kingdom of God. Thus, we see that most children of God that engage in this operate at a different class than others in God's kingdom.

Definition one: Evangelism is the currency needed to claim what we desire in the kingdom of God. So, are you rich or poor in the kingdom?

Stance Two – The Company of God

In a company, there are many departments. Each of these departments has different responsibilities and employs individuals, as needed, to carry out these responsibilities. Among these many departments is a vital one called the human resource department (HR). This department is tasked to oversee every human resource concern (such as hiring) of the company.

Christianity is somewhat like a company founded by three co-founders, God the Father, God the Son — Jesus, and God the Holy Spirit. These founders operate the company together and they all have equal power but are tasked with different responsibilities, so they operate differently.

God the Father is responsible for overseeing the company's performances and operations. Due to the nature of His responsibility, He can be deemed as the Chief Executive Officer (CEO). All major decisions ultimately come from Him. As the CEO, He, therefore, resides in and performs His responsibilities from His office at the headquarters in heaven. He is the Father of all and the God of all (See **Ephesians 4:6**).

Jesus, who is God the Son, is responsible for the expansion of the company. He executes His responsibility by creating the HR and customer service departments where it is needed. The talent acquisition section of the HR department is responsible for hiring people into this company (fold) of God, while the customer service department takes care and helps them with their concerns. In this company of God, however, the HR department hiring is more like an adoption into becoming a child of God.

Now let's zoom into the HR department and drill even deeper. Jesus came into the world to establish this department here on earth, where the harvests are. This is because companies and their branches are strategically situated at the location where their products are needed the most. The company of God's product is salvation—which is basically the promise of rich, satisfying and eternal life (See **John 3:16 & John 10:10**). Through evangelism, people are first saved, then they are recruited into the company of God. Therefore, humans here on earth are the only focus for this product— (the salvation program).

*He said to his disciples, "The harvest is great (here on earth), but the workers are few. (**Matthew 9:37 NLT; emphasis added**)*

To encourage and get more people to want the product, Jesus started by vetting, employing, and training twelve core people (*Disciples or Apostles*) in the HR department (See **Matthew 10:2-4**). During this training, He taught them many things, but love was the major focus. This is because, to get others to sign up for the product (salvation program), love is a necessity. Therefore, since the first twelve employees, love has become a requirement for every company employee to have while carrying out his/her "job" of evangelism.

And you must love the LORD your God with all your heart, all your soul, all your mind, and all your strength. The second is *equally important: 'Love your neighbor as yourself.' No other commandment is greater than these. (**Mark 12:30-31 NLT**)*

After the establishment through Jesus' life, death and resurrection, He left for heaven where He now sits at the right hand of the CEO, advocating for His departmental employees.

*Who then will condemn us? No one--for Christ Jesus died for us and was raised to life for us, and he is sitting in the place of honor at God's right hand, pleading for us. (**Romans 8:34 NLT**)*

Later, Jesus will be needed to transfer His employees out of this earth's office to the headquarters in heaven; non-employees will see death (hell) while the employees will see a promotion and transformation (See **Matthew 24:30-31 & 1 Corinthians 15:52**). Any Christian alive when Jesus returns will experience rapture.

For those that die before this event, Jesus will be standing in heaven to welcome His departmental employees who had done a great job evangelizing—the requirement of the company.

*It will happen in a moment, in the blink of an eye, when the last trumpet is blown. For when the trumpet sounds, those who have died will be raised to live forever. And we who are living will also be transformed. (**1 Corinthians 15:52 NLT**)*

*"The master was full of praise. 'Well done, my good and faithful servant. You have been faithful in handling this small amount, so now I will give you many more responsibilities. Let's celebrate together! (**Matthew 25:21 NLT**)*

"Look," he said, "I see heaven open and the Son of Man standing

at the right hand of God." (Ready to welcome Him) (**Acts 7:56 NLT, Emphasis Added**)

During the life of Jesus, He went around with His twelve "newbies" to make known to people the "new company in town". Many inquired, some applied to the program, and others even got free promo services such as healings and many miracles on the run. However, only twelve and a few others stayed. Jesus left the survival of this departmental office here on earth in the hands of the twelve and with the help of one of the three co-founders, the Holy Spirit who relocated to the earth after Jesus left. This marks the beginning of the era of this third co-founder. To learn more about this third co-founder, I encourage you to read *"The Most Important Person of Our Time" by Ebenezer Agboola.*

But in fact, it is best for you that I go away, because if I don't, the Advocate (the Holy Spirit) won't come. If I do go away, then I will send him to you. (**John 16:7 NLT; emphasis added**)

One of the goals of this department is to increase the company by selling its product to as many as possible. When one of the co-founders, Jesus, was leaving, He made this clear to the twelve disciples and the others who were with them. This is the goal for the current and subsequent employees of this company.

And then he told them, "Go into all the world and preach the Good News to everyone. (**Mark 16:15 NLT**)

We see that from this analogy, even though one of the main tasks of the HR department is to help hire people for the company, it is also the responsibility of this department to hire people who will help with the process of hiring others.

Therefore, it is only a true born-again Christian that is concerned with evangelism. In other words, after we've gotten the product and have been hired, then we are automatically required to hire other people. You don't hire for a company unless you are part of the company's human resource department. If you do, you must have some sort of arrangement with the company, otherwise, it is a fraud. This is the qualification. When we become Christians, which is only through Jesus (See **Romans 10:9-10**), we become part of a department whose goal is to hire more people.

These people will in turn also help in hiring others, and the cycle continues. We are Christians to help others become Christians. This we do through love as instructed by our company's co-founder (Jesus) (see **Mark 12:31**).

Definition two: Evangelism is the process of increasing and hiring more people into the company of God for the purpose of salvation, adoption and relationship with God.

Stance Three – Spiritual Pollination

I am the true grapevine, and my Father is the gardener. He cuts off every branch of mine that doesn't produce fruit, and he prunes the branches that do bear fruit, so they will produce even more. You have already been pruned and purified by the message I have given you. Remain in me, and I will remain in you. For a branch cannot produce fruit if it is severed from the vine, and you cannot be fruitful unless you remain in me. "Yes, I am the vine; you are the branches. Those who remain in me, and I in them, will produce much fruit. For apart from me you can do nothing. Anyone who does not remain in me is thrown away like a useless branch and withers. Such branches are gathered into a pile to be burned. But if you remain in me and my words remain in you, you may ask for anything you want, and it will be granted! When you produce much fruit, you are my true disciples. This brings great glory to my Father. (***John 15:1-8 NLT***)

Christianity can be compared to a grape tree. In this tree, Jesus is the center and the main piece, that is, the trunk which is also the vine for a grape tree. He is the core of the Christianity tree. Everything in the Christianity tree (and in life) is held together by Jesus Christ.

He (Jesus) existed before anything else, and he holds all creation together. (***Colossians 1:17 NLT, emphasis added***)

Jesus told him, "I am the way, the truth, and the life. No one can come to the Father except through me. (***John 14:6 NLT***)

Jesus is life. This simply means that it is through Him that we exist. Without Him we are nothing. Therefore, we are doomed if we do not have or know Jesus.

For in him (Jesus) we live and move and exist. As some of your own poets have said, 'We are his offspring.' (***Acts 17:28 NLT, emphasis added***)

Since Jesus is the trunk and the core of our Christian tree, from Him, branches will grow which in turn will produce the fruit. These fruits give identity to the tree, hence the name apple tree, fig tree, grape tree and many more. The essence of a tree is known by its fruit.

A tree with many branches but no fruits lacks identity and

thereby is useless. Jesus rebuked the fig tree because of its lack of essence. If a tree exists, fruit is expected when needed.

*He noticed a fig tree in full leaf a little way off, so he went over to see if he could find any figs. But there were only leaves because it was too early in the season for fruit. Then Jesus said to the tree, "May no one ever eat your fruit again!" And the disciples heard him say it. (**Mark 11:13-14 NLT**)*

On the Christian tree, the branches are the disciples of Jesus, that is, Christians (see **John 15:5**). We are expected to produce a certain fruit that gives identity to the tree—Jesus. The name Christian was given to the tree whose fruit, the apostles, produced in Antioch. Therefore, our fruits determine the name of the tree.

It was at Antioch that the believers were first called Christians. (**Acts 11:26b NLT**)

God is the planter of this tree, and as such, He expects a certain fruit based on the kind of tree He planted. He is the gardener who prunes the good and cuts out the unwanted and fruitless branches (see **John 15:6**). So, a branch cannot decide its own fruit and cannot produce fruit without the trunk/vine. Therefore, we cannot decide our own fruit, and we cannot produce the right kind of fruit without Jesus.

So, let's discover what fruit is expected from us, the branch?

*For God made Christ, who never sinned, to be the offering for our sin, so that we could be made right with God through Christ. (**2 Corinthians 5:21 NLT**)*

As Christians, we are righteous through Jesus Christ.

There is no condemnation for us (see **Romans 8:1**), but by faith, we are as pure as Jesus. As such, the fruit of the righteous is a tree of life; and he who wins souls is wise (**Proverbs 11:30 NKJV**).

Therefore, if we are righteous, then we belong to the tree of life. And as a branch on this tree, our fruit is therefore life. **Proverbs 11:30** preceded by saying that a wise person will win souls in order to produce this fruit—life. This is because as seen in **Mark 11:13-14** and **John 15:6**, lack of fruit production will lead us to destruction and sever of the branch. A wise branch will produce the fruit of life by winning souls (Evangelism). The truth you know and do not declare can land you in trouble (see **Ezekiel 33:1-6**).

Furthermore, if Jesus is life, as He declared in **John 14:6** and the vine (trunk) of the Christian tree as per **John 15:5**, then the fruit expected from His tree is life.

Since we are expected to produce life as fruit, **Proverbs 11:30** qualify the tree that we, the righteous, belong to as the tree of life. Therefore, one of the essences of the Christian tree is to produce life. For better understanding, let us use the science behind a tree to explain the spiritual meaning of evangelism.

In biology, the process of producing seeds and fruit around it is called pollination. According to the United States Department of Agriculture, pollination is the act of transferring pollen grains from the male anther of a flower to the female stigma. This can be done within the same flower or from another flower. Pollination is needed for fertilization, and fertilization allows the flower to develop seeds. This is the normal pollination of a plant.

The pollen grains are housed within the flower, in a similar way that salvation is housed within God (Jesus). We can compare the flower on the Christian tree to everything we know about God. This is because out of the things that we know about the vine—God (Jesus) is the pollen grain. The salvation message has to be moved/transferred from the anthers. The stigma in our case is the receiver of the message. And there are many kinds of stigma that may be encountered; these are explained in **Luke 8:4-15**.

From this metaphor, we can say that evangelism is the process of generating fruit—life can be known as spiritual pollination. It is the act of moving/spreading/transferring the message of salvation (the pollen grain) from those that are already connected (the anthers) to the lost (the stigma).

From this definition, it is inferred that pollination only occurs between flowers. In the same way, evangelism is a human species occurrence. There are no other species on earth with the need for salvation messages other than humans. So, a person tells another person about salvation through Jesus.

It must be noted that the moment pollination occurs, nature takes over. The moment the pollen grains are transferred and the process of pollination is done, nature kicks in and fertilization, or otherwise, occurs. Similarly, in evangelism, we are the conveyor, not the converter. Once we have shared or moved the salvation message by telling it to another, the next phase becomes the work of the Holy Spirit.

It is not our responsibility to convict or convert. That is the work of the Holy Spirit.

*And when he comes, he will convict the world of its sin, and of God's righteousness, and of the coming judgment. (**John 16:8 NLT**)*

Furthermore, the complexity of individuals explains why evangelism can be a tough thing to do. It is impossible to evangelize effectively without the help of the Holy Spirit. Therefore, evangelism is a partnership between us and the Holy Spirit (See **1 Corinthians 3:9**). We convey and the Holy Spirit convicts. The responsibilities of the Holy Spirit in this process, however, should not be our concern. We should be focused on how to do ours properly and efficiently.

All that is required of us is to move the message. Any deviation (such as argument, contention and so on) is disobedience and therefore a sin. These are a waste of time and tactics of the enemy to get us into sin, off track and not fulfilling the process of pollination. The moment the set process of pollination is interrupted, the purpose is defeated.

*If any household or town refuses to welcome you or listen to your message, shake its dust from your feet as you leave. (**Matthew 10:14 NLT**).*

THE POLLEN GRAINS

From the explanation above, the pollen grains are the salvation message. It is important that for pollen grains to accomplish the aim of fertilization in the stigma and thereby produce fruit, it must contain all the necessary contents and nutrients. In our case, the salvation message we are moving must be rich enough for the next phase with the aim to cause fertilization in a person. This is our responsibility, but rich messages only come from the Holy Spirit, hence the partnership mentioned earlier. This simply means that we must totally depend on the Holy Spirit even for our messages. But there are generic contents expected of every salvation message. These contents will be discussed here. As mentioned earlier, the Holy Spirit holds the absolute right to make modifications as necessary to these messages. He knows the other person more than we think we know. Therefore, it is always a good idea to pray about what we are about to do. Also, we must consult, or be in tune with the Holy Spirit before, after and during the movement of the salvation message.

Once we are saved, we all become existing living branches with leaves/flowers. Leaves/flowers signify everything we know about God. Out of all we know about God is the message that required movement or transfer for fertilization. But for fertilization to occur and for proper fruit production, a complete salvation message (pollen grains) may contain, but are not limited to the following: The purpose of Jesus, your testimony, and how to be saved. Though all these are essential, we must decide the sequence and the needed ones with the help of the Holy Spirit.

The Purpose of Jesus

*And she will have a son, and you are to name him Jesus, for he will save his people from their sins. (**Matthew 1:21 NLT**)*

The Bible verse above shows the message as simple and

precise. The purpose of Jesus is to save us from sin. Jesus was sent out of God's love for humanity.

*"For God loved the world so much that he gave his one and only Son, so that everyone who believes in him will not perish but have eternal life. (**John 3:16 NLT**).*

Humans are created in God's image/nature. I have a cousin who often says, "I am God's selfie". This is true, we are all His selfies. We are the reflection of God's perfection.

*Then God said, "Let us make human beings in our image, to be like us. They will reign over the fish in the sea, the birds in the sky, the livestock, all the wild animals on the earth, and the small animals that scurry along the ground." (**Genesis 1:26 NLT**)*

The plural form of God's statement in the verse of the scripture above shows clearly that God was talking to another Being at the very least. Looking even deeper into this verse, we discovered that God wants to make human beings to be like Himself and the others involved in this conversation. Clearly, we can say God wasn't talking to angels or any of the other beings in heaven; because He was using "us" and "our", so He was speaking to people of His status and calibre (Jesus and the Holy Spirit).

Our God is triune in nature, that is, He is one God who is manifested in three different forms. His forms are God the Father, God the Son (Jesus) and God the Holy Spirit. The divine nature of God makes it very possible for His three manifestations to have a conversation as that of three individuals. So, in **Genesis 1:26**, the Father, who created all things (see **Genesis 1:1**) was talking to the Son—Jesus and the Holy Spirit. He was saying "Hey guys, let us make humans three-in-one beings the way we are". Therefore, we are the only beings with this very similar triune nature of God. This demonstrates the extremity of the unconditional love of God for us. The form of our nature is spirit, soul, and body. To better understand God and human trinity nature, I encourage you to read *"The Person You Should Know" by Ebenezer Agboola.*

Our physical representation here on earth is the body, we were made alive by the breath of God (see **Genesis 2:7**). Therefore, our spirit was created from the breath of God and our soul houses everything we are (our will, emotion and intellect). What defines our actions and reactions are stored up in the soul; this was why Jesus lay emphasis on the soul in **Matthew 16:26.** Once we die, the body is buried here, the spirit leaves the body and serves as a body for the soul in the spiritual realm. God will then judge the soul based on our belief system. (see **2 Corinthians 5:10** and **Hebrews 9:27**).

In **Genesis 2:7**, we see that we are made alive by the breath of God. But the breath of God obviously longs for Him. The moment Adam and Eve ate the fruit and sinned, they brought sin to us all. Every person is separated from God; so, the longing for God in us became disconnected from its source. Also, remember how I mentioned that we are God's selfie? This means when God sees us, He rejoices. God is always happy to see us because He sees Himself in us. The moment sin entered; the image God sees became covered up with sin.

Over different dispensations, we have tried many ways to fill our thirst for God. We tried filling it with other things such as idols, but nothing can take the place of God, except

God. This human struggle was real to God, so He decided to take several approaches, based on His timetable over different dispensations. But our sin problem makes us so weak, that we cannot possibly survive, adhere to, or even comprehend this different salvation approaches.

The love for humanity then propelled God to come for us in the form of Jesus. Just as you would do to save your pet or child in a hole/ditch, God jumped into the pit of sin to save us.

Another important point here is, contrary to some beliefs, the love of God for humans is the utmost reason for Jesus. Yes, hell is real, but it is not the main reason for the coming of Jesus. God made hell for the devil and His angels. Not for humans.

*Then the King will turn to those on the left and say, 'Away with you, you cursed ones, into the eternal fire prepared for the devil and his demons. (**Matthew 25:41 NLT**)*

So, when God was thinking about His salvation plan, His love was the motivation, not the meanness and the horror of hell. However, whoever is not saved through Jesus has chosen the devil and will have to go to the place God has made for the devil. God obviously doesn't want us there, hence why hell is not the main reason for salvation through Jesus.

So, the love of God is the main reason for sending Jesus and His main purposes are to save us from sin, hell and restore our relationship with God.

Our Testimony

Many Samaritans from the village believed in Jesus because the woman had said, "He told me everything I ever did!' (***John 4:39 NLT***)

Our testimony is another part of the message to be transferred. This verse of the scripture was from a popular story where a woman who was deemed a sinner at the time because of her lifestyle, ended up bringing the awareness of Jesus, the savior to her community. This she did with her testimony. Sometimes, all that is needed to effectively evangelize is the act of sharing other people's or our own experiences. Everyone responds more easily to a person who has been through the same ordeal. It gives the sense of "oh, he/she understands me". Naturally, people are more open to whoever they believe understands them and can help them. For example, if God has saved you from a situation, sickness or disease that a person is struggling with, sharing such testimony with them could help them decide to seek God. The Samaritans believed because of the woman's testimony. So, we really have no excuse not to share our testimony, unless God, through Jesus hasn't really done anything for us. Let us share our testimonies and not worry about how funny or maybe embarrassing it might look or sound. If it is embarrassing such as our life before we were transformed by Jesus, then we must remember that it is in the past and old things have passed away (see **2 Corinthians 5:17**).

Also, testimonies are powerful and effective tools in the hand of God. This is because God is a miracle worker, not a magician. There is a difference between the two. A magician doesn't really need anything from you. It is a form of entertainment, that might help or not help anybody. But the essence of it is to show off and possibly make some profit in doing so. A miracle worker, on the other hand, needs something (no matter how small) from us to perform a miracle. Miracles are displayed for the sole purpose of making the impossible possible to help people know and believe in God. Miracles are never for show or profit, they are to ease people from their pain. Genuine miracles come from God and therefore are not forced on you without your willingness. So, the miracle worker will require your participation to confirm your willingness. He uses what you have, to perform the miracle you need. All the miracles of Jesus show the true definition of miracles. So, the two things that define miracles are the desire of the seeker and the necessity of the miracle.

In **Matthew 14:13-21,** Jesus fed over five thousand people. He did not show off, He did it because it was necessary. Jesus is God and as such, He doesn't really need the five loaves and two fishes to create more food. The person they got this from was a point of contact to the crowd. Whoever released that bread and fish, gave consent for the willingness. Though the crowd might not be seeking a miracle, they were clearly hungry or would eventually become hungry. Jesus was moved by compassion and sought out the willingness to bring about miracles. But as per the nature of miracles, without the inclination of the miracle seeker, there will be no miracle.

Another perfect example to confirm this doctrine is Jesus' first miracle. This was from **John 2:1-11**; Jesus turned water into wine when He was approached for help after the wine was finished. Jesus requested that water be fetched and He, in turn, changed the water to wine miraculously. First of all, like every other miracle, there was a need for it. Secondly, Jesus needed to make sure of the willfulness, hence the request for water. These are the two ingredients for miracles.

For most miracles, Jesus would often ask what can I do for you? Though in most cases it was quite clear that the person needed help with his sight or something like that (see **John 18**). Jesus was doing this to confirm their willingness. The necessity is there, but the desire must be confirmed.

The truth is, soul-winning is a miracle that only God can perform, hence the need to rely on the Holy Spirit. We must understand that the need for soul winning is there; many are destined to go to hell because they do not know Jesus. This is a heartbreak for God and not His plan.

*He said to his disciples, "The harvest is great, but the workers are few. (**Matthew 9:37 NLT**).*

We are the designated miracle seeker; therefore, by sharing our testimony, we are given God a form of confirmation for our willingness. Just as spreading the message about Jesus is important; so, it is that we surrender what we have for the miracle of soul winning that we seek.

*And then he told them, "Go into all the world and preach the Good News to everyone. (**Mark 16:15 NLT**).*

Even though our testimonies are very important, including them in evangelism is not our call, but that of the Holy Spirit. This is because sharing things about ourselves could get some people off the hinge and not want to listen. Also, if care is not taken and/or not done properly, we can easily drift into pride; which is something God hates and hence sin. So, it is therefore important to consult with the Holy Spirit on this very point. He knows everything and everyone and can help us to devise the right approach.

How to Be Saved

This is the last necessary content of the pollen grains and it is based on Romans chapter 10, verses 9 to 10:

If you confess with your mouth that Jesus is Lord and believe in your heart that God raised him from the dead, you will be saved. For it is by believing in your heart that you are made right with God, and it is by confessing with your mouth that you are saved. (**Romans 10:9-10 NLT**)

From the verses above, we can deduce that two things must be done to be saved. These are confessing and believing. Now, let us break these down for proper understanding.

Believing: This is a heart thing. It is the foundation of what is confessed. In fact, this is done first before we can truly confess.

"For God loved the world so much that he gave his one and only Son, so that everyone who believes in him will not perish but have eternal life. (**John 3:16 NLT**)

We believe in our heart to connect and make things right with God while we confess Jesus to let the world and the devil know that we are now a child of God.

In **Proverbs 23:7 NKJV** that *for as he thinks in his heart,* *so is he.* The Bible described us as the content of our hearts. So, we see that we must first be convinced in our heart of the salvation work of Jesus. Therefore, our belief is the very foundation of our salvation. Our transformation is based on this foundation.

Confession only affirm what has already taken place in us because *whatever is in our heart determines what you say* (**Matthew 12:34 NLT**)

Confessing: When a baby is born, it is important and a necessity that he/she cries to signify to the world of his/her entry. In the same way, confession is a necessity for a new spiritual birth. To confess Jesus as Lord will require a certain understanding of Him. Any confession of Jesus without a thorough understanding of His salvation work is a waste of time, hence the need to know the purpose of Jesus. Jesus saves us from sin—this means that for us to come to Jesus, we must realize that we are sinners in need of help. As I have explained earlier, we see that in many encounters of Jesus, He asked people, "what can I do for you?" Though Bartimaeus called Jesus by name, admitting the need for Him, Jesus still asked him that same question (See **Mark 10:46-52**). So, when we come to Jesus, we must tell Him why we have come. That is, to confess our sin and receive Him as our Lord and Savior.

But if we confess our sins to him, he is faithful and just to forgive us our sins and to cleanse us from all wickedness. (**1 John 1:9 NLT**)

Until we renounce sin and ask for forgivingness, by making Jesus our Lord, sin oversees and rules our life. As the lord of our life, we do what we are asked to do by sin. We must renounce being ruled by sin and instead accept the Lordship of Jesus.

"No one can serve two masters. For you will hate one and love the other; you will be devoted to one and despise the other. You cannot serve both God and money (sin)." (**Luke 16:13 NLT, emphasis added**)

Since these two are important for salvation, it is important to do these two together and in the name of Jesus who rescued us and made all this possible. Hence the need for Sinner's Prayer. Ideally, every sinner coming to God will pray this prayer. Since prayer is only done effectively by believing (See **Mark 11:24**), these prayer envelopes both the necessities of confession and believing. However, this prayer must be prayed aloud to fulfil the requirement of confession. So, it is advisable that this prayer be recited by the soon-to-be, newly spiritual born. Below is a typical sample of the Sinner's Prayer.

Sample Sinner's Prayer

*Father in the name of Jesus, thank You for sending Your Son Jesus Christ to die on the cross for my sins. I know that I am a sinner who has sinned against you. According to your word in **1 John 1:9**, I hereby confess my sins to You; please forgive my sins and wash me from all my iniquities. Since you died for me on the cross in the form of God the Son—Jesus Christ; I, therefore, confess Jesus Christ as my personal Lord and savior. From this day forward, I surren-*

der myself under the leadership of your Holy Spirit and I will forever do your will, my Lord, so help me God, Amen.

The day this or a variation of this prayer is said is our spiritual birthday, which is the day we become born again. So, it is important to note this day for our record.

Evangelists-The Office

*Now, these are the gifts Christ gave to the church: the apostles, the prophets, the **evangelists**, and the pastors and teachers. (**Ephesians 4:11 NLT**)*

Among the five-fold ministry stated in the scripture above, is the evangelist. Google defines an evangelist as a person who seeks to convert others to the Christian faith, especially by public preaching. There is no way we will discuss evangelism without talking about this office. Though from our definitions, we see that every Christian is required to evangelize, where does the evangelist fit in? Or are all Christians in the office of evangelists? The answer to the latter question is no, not all Christians are called to be evangelists. But there is a big part for the office of an evangelist in Christendom.

As their name implies and from the google definition, an evangelist's sole job is to convey the message of salvation to unbelievers. Once this seed is planted, there is a chance their job is done. This is all they do. In this office, all they care about is the lost souls. They strive, cry and pray for the lost. They are eager, compassionate, energetic and willing to go to any length to get that message to the lost souls. This is their drive and motivation.

On the other hand, you and I, who are not predominantly in this office, do it as a part of the requirement for our Christianity. I say this because any of God's commands is a requirement for our Christianity. This might not be our drive, so it may not even be our call, but we are required to do it. Therefore, we do it as led by God. For example, it is the job of a soldier to adhere to commands, laws and protocols. But it is a requirement for a civilian to obey the law. But for a soldier, this is at a whole different level. In the same vein, it is the job of an accountant to understand and be able to figure out finances and taxes, but it is a requirement for you and I to file our taxes and keep relevant documents. So, in the same way, it is the job of an evangelist to convey the salvation message, but for other Christians, the command in **Mark 16:15-16** makes this a requirement for our salvation.

Once the evangelist plants the seed, and a harvest is made, the subsequent step could then be one of our own primary callings. For example, once a soul comes to Christ and starts attending the church, the responsibility of the growth of such individuals now becomes that of the church and the pastor.

Remember, all these offices and gifts constitute the body of Christ. Therefore, we are parts of one body, working together (See **1 Corinthians 12**).

2

Reasons for the Act

In chapter 1, we learned about the stances of God on evangelism, but why is evangelism so important today? It is often said that "those that know the how will always work for those that know the why". The why of a thing reveals the importance of that thing. It is true because the understanding of the importance of a thing often gives the motivation and insight needed to achieve the aim; thus, the necessity of this chapter. There are a few reasons why evangelism is important and necessary in Christianity.

To Fulfil the Plan of God

As Christians, we understand that one of the main reasons for our existence here on earth is to fulfil the plan of God. We are God's extension here on earth (see **Psalm 82:6** and **John 10:34**), we are His ambassadors, and as such we should seek His interest. When God made us, He gave us dominion (See **Genesis 1:26**). As such, the earth is our domain/territory because we are alive. It is simply impossible for neither God nor the devil to achieve certain things here on earth without humans. So, for every fulfilled plan of God on earth, there is/are human(s) involved. My father in the Lord (Pastor EA Adewusi) once said to me "the plans of God do not change, but the people involved can change." This simply means that we are not an indispensable factor when it comes to God's plan here on earth. Yes, without humanity, God's plans are left hanging in the balance, however, if a person refuses God, another will be ready to say yes to God.

*Then God said, "Let us make human beings in our image, to be like us. They will reign over the fish in the sea, the birds in the sky, the livestock, all the wild animals on the earth, and the small animals that scurry along the ground." (**Genesis 1:26 NLT**)*

*So, we are Christ's ambassadors; God is making his appeal (on earth) through us. We speak for Christ when we plead, "Come back to God!" (**2 Corinthians 5:20 NLT, emphasis added**)*

*He said to his disciples, "The harvest is great, but the workers are few. (**Matthew 9:37 NLT**)*

Since the fall of man, God's plan has always been to unite us with Himself in heaven, once our journey on earth is over. He wants our souls back at home in heaven, so we can be with Him for eternity (see **Philippians 3:20**). God, like every parent, derives joy in the company of His children. Hence the reason for joy in heaven over a sinner that comes to God (see **Luke 15:7**), and the joy experienced when we are in the presence of God. God is enthroned when we are in His presence (see **Psalm 22:3**) and as such, we experience the joy of the Lord in the presence of the Lord (see **Psalm 16:11**).

*There is more than enough room in my Father's home. If this were not so, would I have told you that I am going to prepare a place for you? (**John 14:2 NLT**)*

The many rooms in heaven are because of the expectations of the builder of heaven. God expects us all to come back to Him after death. However, the enemy is fighting to keep these rooms vacant and empty; this will make the preparation of Jesus futile.

The truth is, if there is any chance for heaven to be filled and fulfil God's plan, we are the ones that will help populate heaven through evangelism. Once we are transported by death, neither our spiritual being nor the angels can do this. We are alive now, this is our time and our domain, we are the ones here to serve God by evangelizing.

*"Then the rich man said, 'Please, Father Abraham, at least send him to my father's home. For I have five brothers, and I want him to warn them, so they don't end up in this place of torment.' "But Abraham said, 'Moses and the prophets have warned them. Your brothers can read what they wrote.'"The rich man replied, 'No, Father Abraham! But if someone is sent to them from the dead, then they will repent of their sins and turn to God.' **"But Abraham said, 'If they won't listen to Moses and the prophets, they won't be persuaded even if someone rises from the dead.'"** (**Matthew 16:27-31 NLT**)*

A Very Important Command

A true Christian (an individual who has a relationship

with God) is the one who should seek to be like Jesus day by day. Our goal in life is to be like Him in acts and in deeds.

Those who say they live in God should live their lives as Jesus did. (***1 John 2:6 NLT***)

To achieve this, obedience is needed and very essential. We cannot please God or be like Jesus unless we obey the commands and instructions given to us by God.

But Samuel replied, "What is more pleasing to the LORD: your burnt offerings and sacrifices or your obedience to his voice? Listen! Obedience is better than sacrifice, and submission is better than offering the fat of rams. (***1 Samuel 15:22 NLT***)

Jesus is our leader; we look up to Him in everything. Just like any follower, obeying the instructions of the leader is our utmost responsibility. In our case, we must obey the commands of Jesus. All the commands of God are created to model us like Jesus. This is because He (Jesus) is the only God who lived on earth in flesh. So, the more we obey these commands, the more we are being shaped into the image of Jesus. The one we obey we become.

If you love me, obey my commandments. (***John 14:15 NLT***)

Furthermore, as seen in the scripture above, obedience is the proof of the love we have towards God (Jesus).

Therefore, go and make disciples of all the nations, baptizing them in the name of the Father and the Son and the Holy Spirit. (***Matthew 28:19 NLT***)

The instruction in the scripture above was the last command that Jesus gave to both the twelve disciples and to us, the future ones as Christians. Many might say because Jesus was talking directly to His twelve disciples at the time, then maybe the command wasn't meant for the new disciples—believers of today. The truth is, all the commands of Jesus were both for that time and are prophecies for today and the future. Therefore, all of Jesus' words and acts are still relevant even today.

I believe that Jesus kept this command until His last moments on earth for a reason. He wanted His disciples to take this command seriously and understand its importance. This command set the tone and became the mission statement of the disciples.

Naturally, we tend to pay more attention to the last word or wishes of a dying person. We believe whatever it is that they are willing to say must be very important. According to the accounts of Mark in **Mark 16:19**, our savior—Jesus ascended to heaven right after giving this instruction. Though Jesus is still alive today, He is seated at the right hand of the Father. We can say the circumstances surrounding this instruction are synonymous with the last word/wish of a dying man in our world.

Also, every company exists for some form of gain. These gains are often what become the visions that are pursued by the employees. We are now employees in the company of God and our main vision is to expand the kingdom by winning more souls. Jesus explained the scope of the vision and the challenges we will face. So, the moment we become a follower of Jesus, we ought to work to accomplish this very important calling. The level of importance that Jesus laid on this only reveals that it is one of our most important commands. Spreading the good news of the love of God through Jesus is one of the main priorities for Christianity.

*He said to his disciples, "The harvest is great, but the workers are few. (**Matthew 9:37 NLT**)*

Therefore, evangelism is not just one of Jesus's commands, but a very important one. It is the foundation of the current phase of Christianity—after the physical existence of Jesus phase. And to sustain this new phase, this is the command that must be obeyed.

The Danger of Hell

The highway to hell is sin. However, the word sin is an envelope word-covering for many bad things that we can do. Sin is anything that we do that violates any of the commands given to us by God. Therefore, from our previous discussion, we can say that not evangelizing is a sin. But how?

And then he told them, "Go into all the world and preach the Good News to everyone. Anyone who believes and is baptized will be saved. But anyone who refuses to believe will be condemned. (**Mark 16:15-16 NLT**).

From the scripture above, it is very clear that evangelism is a command of Jesus to us all. Any follower of Jesus who decided not to do it will be violating this command of God. This is therefore disobedience; such a person would have sinned and will end up in hell if they don't repent and amend their ways with God.

From the second stance in chapter 1, this is only one of

the many departments, in the company of God, that was established here on earth. Jesus established this department, as the human resource department. This implies that everyone hired by this department here on earth is hired for the sake of hiring others. This is the only goal of this department. Not doing this only means we are employed to do a job and we are not performing our duties, and we can be fired. However, being fired in this case will mean being taken out of the company of God which is basically relapsing back to sin, hence the possibility of hell (See **Matthew 3:10**).

This department was established here because there were and are still many souls to harvest here on earth (See **Matthew 9:37**), and it is our responsibility to reap all the harvests. So, let's get to the work that we were employed to do.

Also, the third stance from chapter 1 gives another insight into the possibility of hell. From **John 15:1-8** we can deduce that the only condition to remain as part of the vine is fruit production. This is something required of us for as long as we want to be part of the vine. It is therefore a constant cycle that never stops until our death. In other words, it is something that must keep happening. We also find from the previous chapter that the only way to produce the fruit that keeps us with the vine is evangelism. The moment we stop, we are going down a dangerous road of being cut off and getting burned (See **John 15:5-6**). We must keep in mind that this verse of the Bible is a parable of Jesus, which I believe meant that getting burned was used to connote the fact that it is possible to miss heaven if we do not produce fruit. This is because once the branch that represents us is cut off, we will have no relationship with the vine (God). And with a lack of a relationship with God, hell is inevitable.

Saved and Preserved for this very Act

But the other criminal protested, "Don't you fear God even when you have been sentenced to die? We deserve to die for our crimes, but this man hasn't done anything wrong." Then he said, "Jesus, remember me when you come into your Kingdom". And Jesus replied, "I assure you, today you will be with me in paradise." (**Luke 23:40-43 NLT**).

Have you ever wondered why we are still here on earth after being saved? This is a question that the thief on the cross from the Bible verse above never had to ask. His situation was unique and special. He made it to heaven right after salvation. But this is not true for everyone and if you are a Christian reading this, then this is not true for you either.

Also, to those who believed that the only reason to become a Christian is just to make heaven, this is not just wrong, but a misguided notion. Heaven is part of the packages of Christianity, but not the only reason. It cost God nothing to take us out of this world right after salvation. He did this for the thief on the cross.

The particular heaven that Jesus promised in **John 14:2-3**, and making it there is an after-life event. It is quite different from the one Jesus spoke about in **Luke 17:21**. This is the one that will happen once our time here on earth is over. In this experience, we will be where Jesus is. This sounds like a very good deal. So, if that's the case, why does God leave us alive here on earth? What's the reason for our preservation in this world after being saved?

God keeps us here to evangelize to others or gather the harvests, so to speak. That is, to obey God and be blessed in the process. Many people are concerned about getting to heaven but do not care about what they have in heaven. This is important because if you are a child of God, saved by Jesus, and continue to walk with God, then you will make heaven. But heaven is like every other destination other than the fact that God lives in heaven. The life you will have in heaven comes from only those things that you have stored up in heaven based on your activities here on earth (See **Matthew 6:19**). In other words, our terrestrial life determines this extraterrestrial life.

We have established that evangelism helps our life here on earth (See **John 15:7**). Obeying God's instructions opens gates to various blessings. But how does evangelism help our life eternally? Evangelism is one of God's ways for us to store up treasures in heaven.

*"Don't store up treasures here on earth, where moths eat them, and rust destroys them, and where thieves break in and steal. Store your treasures in heaven, where moths and rust cannot destroy, and thieves do not break in and steal. Wherever your treasure is, there the desires of your heart will also be. (**Matthew 6:19-21 NLT**)*

Because evangelism is an important commandment the treasure stored in heaven from this act will be more than other commandments. As established previously, if we die without doing this job, then we are heading for hell and as such we are entitled to no reward. In the employment world, as we know it, a person who was hired but quit or never did the job would not be entitled to the salary or the gratuities and benefits that come with that employment. The same is applicable here; if we die after being saved without evangelizing, then we are not entitled to any of the blessings of evangelism here on earth and eternally hell may be inevitable.

Additionally, our works here on earth will be tested by fire in heaven (See **1 Corinthians 3:11**). This works will include evangelism because the scripture said we are to build solely on the foundation of Jesus. Salvation for all is an important reason for Jesus, and evangelism is the main way to build on this foundation. Without savings in our evangelism bank, our work might not make it through this test. But our evangelism savings like other savings will only increase with time; this is, therefore, another reason for us to remain here on earth after being saved.

*For no one can lay any foundation other than the one we already have--Jesus Christ. (**1 Corinthians 3:11 NLT**)*

*But on the judgment day, fire will reveal what kind of work each builder has done. The fire will show if a person's work has any value. (**1 Corinthians 3:13 NLT**)*

There is Rejoicing in Heaven

Considering the tremendous differences between us and God, we can assume that there are virtually very few things that we can do to impress God. God made us, and He knows everything there is about us. There is no way for us to possibly surprise Him.

In our reasoning, making God happy is simply impossible. But we know that if there is rejoicing in a house, then the head of that house must be in a very good mood. God is the head of heaven and if there is rejoicing in heaven, then God must be in a good mood. But what can be the cause of this good mood of God?

In the same way, there is more joy in heaven over one lost sinner who repents and returns to God than over ninety-nine others who are righteous and haven't strayed away! (**Luke 15:7 NLT**)

Yes, one of the purposes of Jesus here on earth was to reveal to us the things going on in heaven. To show us the true nature of our Father and His habitat—heaven. He did this to get us to know our God for who He is rather than the lies that the devil had told and is telling us about Him— deception. For example, Jesus told us about how God's house in heaven can harbor as many of us as possible and He is preparing the place for us (see **John 14:2**). He wants us to know how to please God, and how to make Him happy. In other words, He was telling us the secrets about how to make our Father happy. Naturally, when a father is happy, the children will have unrestricted access to many blessings.

We are created in God's image and as such, happiness, which is often a reaction to good happenings, is food for our soul. When we are happy, it is as if we are intoxicated. To put this into proper perspective, God does certain things for all of us regardless of our faith and beliefs (see **Matthew 5:45**); this He does for us all regardless of His mood (sad or happy). In fact, many times He is there for us even in the situations where we are causing Him sadness—when we sin (See

Romans 5:8). Now imagine what He would do when He is happy and pleased with us. I am sure there are no limits to what He would be ready to do for anyone who makes Him happy. This is one of the reasons why evangelism is key to many good things.

*But if you remain in me and my words remain in you, you may ask for anything you want, and it will be granted! (**John 15:7 NLT**)*

The happiness of God can encourage God to give us our heart desires. The deal that we have with God is for Him to grant all our needs, provided we meet the stipulated conditions (see **Matthew 6:31-32** and **Philippians 4:19**). In other words, as Christians, we should never lack our necessities. However, according to the Bible verse above, it is possible to get to a level where our desires and wants can be met as well. This level will be equivalent to having the power of attorney on behalf of God here on earth. But how do we get to this stage? We must remain in God for that to happen. However, the only condition to remain in God is to produce fruit—evangelism (see **John 15:2**). So, we see evangelism makes God happy and He, in turn, gives us the power of attorney on His behalf here on earth.

Enhance Holiness Living

One of the things that we pursue every day as Christian is to please our Father in heaven. When we please God through our life, then we can approach God easily and be guaranteed heaven after our life here is over.

Work at living in peace with everyone, and work at living a *holy life, for those who are not holy will not see the Lord. (**Hebrews 12:14 NLT**)*

From the Bible verse above, we can deduce that it is through holy living that we can please God. When we please God, we can see Him. Being a churchgoer does not guarantee you heaven, but holy living after being saved is what does. In other words, we must learn to maintain our Christianity. If not, we will lose the essence, value and/or lose heaven altogether (See **Philippians 2:12**). The word Christianity was derived from Christ which is synonymous with Jesus, who is holy according to all records and that of the Bible (See **2 Corinthians 5:21**). And we ought to imitate Jesus and be like Him (See **1 John 2:6**), so a holy life is not an option but a must for Christians.

We have established the need for holiness, but this knowledge is valueless unless we understand the true meaning of holiness. For many years, Christianity had been hit with a series of heresies and wrong theories and deceptive teachings of holiness. It has become one of those concepts that have been misread, misunderstood, mistaught and misinterpreted. This is because of the value and necessity of holiness. The devil understands that once this concept is not well understood—deception, it becomes legalism (rituals); hence dragging people to hell instead of heaven.

Due to the very thin line and extremely possible similarities between holiness and legalism. I will like to explain these two before we proceed.

HOLINESS

*Work hard to show the results of your salvation, obeying God with deep reverence and fear. (**Philippians 2:12b NLT**)*

Paul, the apostle was encouraging us in the scriptures above to basically live a holy life that is pleasing to God. He often does this in his letters as inspired by the Holy Spirit. However, there is a distinction here that separates this instruction from the others. From the first part, he was saying that we must keep on with our salvation and produce results; but the only result that salvation can produce is holy living. It is through this living that we are separated and set apart for God. Another way to put this is that holy living is the result of Christianity.

Apostle Paul proceeds by saying the only way to produce the right result out of our salvation is by obeying God with deep reverence and fear. Therefore, holiness is simply to obey God with deep reverence and fear.

Many believe that holiness is the act of being sinless, this is not just wrong but misleading and therefore a deception that leads to legalism. This is easy to deem right because God has a sinless nature, and this nature defines Him as holy.

However, obeying God is equivalent to being sinless. This is because, each time you obey God, you escape from or repent of sin. This will in turn make you sinless at that point in time. You are clean now, and God does not see you as a sinner anymore; instead, He sees Jesus, who is sinless. (See **1 John 1:9**, **Psalm 103:12** & **Hebrews 8:12**).

LEGALISM

*So, don't let anyone condemn you for what you eat or drink, or for not celebrating certain holy days or new moon ceremonies or Sabbaths. For these rules are only shadows of the reality yet to come. And Christ himself is that reality. (**Colossians 2:16-17 NLT**).*

Many of us have been made to believe that to be holy, we must act and/or behave in a certain way. This is true for the most part because as Christians, there are standards required from us by God and other people. However, the moment these standards become our focus rather than God Himself, then we are in legalism. Our focus as Christians is not to count the number of sins we avoided or committed, but to love and pay very good attention to God, His words and obey all thoroughly to the best of our ability. Joseph said *how then can I do this great wickedness, and sin against God?* (**Genesis 39:9 NKJV**)

Legalism is the act of focusing on a set of standards of any kind to please God and/or humans, which is equivalent to law. For example, when the law of Moses was given, the focus was to get the people clean enough to approach God, the Father who tended to appear on earth tangibly at the time. This was done because the Father was the God of that dispensation and as such a human who is a sinner could come in close proximity with God. As we all know, God is holy and human by nature is not. Therefore, to avoid death during contact, a level of physical and spiritual cleansing is required; thus, the need for those laws as standards to aid the cleansing process. But today, this is not necessary anymore because we approach God the Father through Jesus and we hear and communicate with God through the Holy Spirit. These two appearances of God have made the cleansing process easy for us to approach God; they have consolidated all the previous ways into this simple one.

*"Don't misunderstand why I have come. I did not come to abolish the law of Moses or the writings of the prophets. No, I came to accomplish (consolidate) their purpose. (**Matthew 5:17 NLT; emphasis added**)*

This makes absolute sense because the reason for the law was to get us clean enough to approach God, but Jesus through His death and resurrection opened the door to the staircase of the Holy Spirit. Then the Holy Spirit in turn cleanses us step by step as we approach God, the Father and hence fulfilling the law (See **Hebrews 10:19**).

Jesus said in **John 14:15** and **John 14:23** that obedience comes because of love. And in the process of consolidating the law of Moses, Jesus gave a new law that confirms that love is the fulfilment of the law (See **Romans 13:10**).

Therefore, we can conclude that holiness is obedience, and love is the reason for obedience. So, the foundation of holiness is love. Legalism on the other hand is done out of fear and not love. Anything today done out of fear, rather than love, is not from God (See **1 John 4:18** and **2 Timothy 1:7**). This is why there are as many as 365 "fear not" statements in the King James Version of the Bible.

One of the teachers of religious law was standing there listening to the debate. He realized that Jesus had answered well, so he asked, "Of all the commandments, which is the most important?" Jesus replied, "The most important commandment is this: 'Listen, O Israel! The Lord our God is the one and only Lord. And you must love the Lord your God with all your heart, all your soul, all your mind, and all your strength. The second is equally important: 'Love your neighbor as yourself.' No other commandment is greater than these." (**Mark 12:28-31 NLT**)

Now that we have defined holiness and legalism, let us continue on with our studies. When we evangelize, we feel obligated to live up to our words. We desire this to avoid being a hypocrite and thereby mocked by the very ones we are trying to win for God. This consciousness in our spirit is the benefit that comes with evangelism. Imagine evangelizing to a colleague or neighbor, we will try our best to be cautious and be a good representative of our preaching whenever we see this person. So, if this person is with us at all times, then we become aware of our actions, reactions, and behaviors at all times, as it should be. This will then push us to obey God and His words at all times. So, if we evangelize to everyone around us, then we are more likely to put ourselves in a good environment that will help us live holy—obey God.

Brings Glory to God

*When you produce much fruit, you are my true disciples. This brings great glory to my Father. (**John 15:8 NLT**)*

The pride of every parent is to see that their children are succeeding. For the most part of our life and existence, it has always been God who has always done things for us. We are the ones proud of God because of His faithfulness and all that He has done, doing, and will do for us. However, do you know that evangelism is one of those few things that we can do that makes God become proud of us?

Based on our previous explanation, one way to interpret the Bible verse above is that the moment you evangelize and produce fruit—life, you identify yourself as my disciple and this ultimately brings glory to God". The sad truth is that not every Christian identifies themselves as Jesus's disciples. Many only know God for what they can get from Him and nothing more, another probable reason for the denial in **Matthew 7:22**. If people around you cannot define you as a Christian in word and in deed, then you are not. Evangelism is one of those many ways that we get to identify with Jesus. If you cannot do this in any of the ways that will be explored in Chapter 3, it simply means that you are ashamed of Him. And I assure you that this is another fast way to hell.

*If anyone is ashamed of me and my message, the Son of Man will be ashamed of that person when he returns in his glory and in the glory of the Father and the holy angels. (**Luke 9:26 NLT**)*

Identifying with Jesus as His disciple is a form of advertisement and as such you are the image of Jesus. Due to this fact, there are proper ways to evangelize, as we will explore in the subsequent chapter. Our personalities, testimonies, and representations are all that people have, to decide for or against God. Many will never open the Bible, but they are looking at us, the so-called "children of God". In the world today, many things such as talking about Jesus, have become restricted rather than a necessity. Many nations that used to be on the Lord's side, have decided to accept all, maybe in fear of offending/segregating some. All this makes it very hard for many so-called Christians to stick out their head for God in this hostile world environment. Wherefore, you can imagine how doing this ("the impossible") will make God become proud of us and ultimately bring glory to God.

3

Types and Methods

According to **Jeremiah 16:16**, there are two primary different types of evangelism. You are either evangelizing as a fisherman or a hunter. To be effective, everyone who wants to evangelize should function in these two capacities. A believer who is able to operate as a hunter and fisherman is a skilled sower.

*"Behold, I will send for many **fishermen**," says the Lord, "and they shall fish them, and afterward I will send for many **hunters**, and they shall hunt them from every mountain and every hill, and out of the holes of the rocks"* (***Jeremiah 16:16 NKJV***).

Fishing

One of the ways we sow seeds is by being part of a fishing crew. The composition of a fishing crew can range from two people to an unlimited number of people. When you are a part of an enterprise to share the gospel of Jesus Christ, you are fishing with a fishing crew. Jesus told Peter, *"Follow Me, and I will make you fishers of men"* (**Matthew 4:19 NKJV**).

Jesus Christ sent out His disciples to go and fish for unbelievers. They went out in pairs to share the gospel.

*After these things, the Lord appointed seventy others also and sent them two by two before His face into every city and place where He Himself was about to go. Then He said to them, the harvest truly is great, but the laborers are few; therefore, pray the Lord of the harvest to send out laborers into His harvest. (**Luke 10:1-2 NKJV**)*

A fishing expedition can be small-scale or large-scale. It can be mass evangelism (like in **Acts 2**) or modest expeditions (like that of Paul and Silas). A crusade is an example of fishing. It requires a different set of skills and approaches.

In order to be successful, a fishing crew must have humility and teamwork. We will take a closer look into each characteristic for better understanding.

HUMILITY

One of the most vital characteristics a successful fishing crew needs is humility. Humility is what enables the team to work together. The Bible tells us to, *"Submit ourselves to one another in the fear of God"* (**Ephesians 5:21 NKJV**).

Because this type of evangelism is a joint effort, the team members must be humble for the team to be cohesive. In order for the crew members to submit to their leader, they have to be humble.

Anything with more than one head is a monster. For a fishing crew to be successful, there has to be a leader who the crew is fully convinced is called and empowered by God. Once they are convinced, they should submit to the authority of the leader, in order for the fishing expedition to be successful. The leader should also ensure that every member of the fishing crew, that will be directly involved in the exercise, is chosen by God.

Humility also extends to the leader, as he/she will have to be able to receive advice from the crew members in their own areas of expertise. From the scriptures, we noticed that Jesus Christ was humble enough that He often asked His disciples for advice every now and then. Though, in most cases like the scene in **John 6**, He knew exactly what He had to do. I believe that if the disciple at any of these times, had given a sound suggestion, He would have obliged. In **Matthew 16:22**, we saw Peter rebuking Jesus. Again, this is an indication that Jesus was humble in His relationship with the disciples; therefore, Peter thought he could rebuke Him. A good crew leader does mean you can ask your crew members for insight. However, the ultimate decision rests with the leader.

TEAM WORK

The fishing crew has to be able to work together as a team. Just like a healthy human body, every member of the fishing crew must know the role that they play in the team. No one must seek to exalt themselves above the others. An illustration in the Bible paints a perfect picture of a successful fishing crew.

Blow the trumpet in Zion, and sound an alarm in My holy mountain! Let all the inhabitants of the land tremble; for the day of the Lord is coming, for it is at hand: a day of darkness and gloominess, A day of clouds and thick darkness, like the morning clouds spread over the mountains. **A people come, great and strong**, *the like of whom has never been; nor will there ever be any such after them, even for many successive generations. A fire devours before them, and behind them a flame burns; the land is like the Garden of Eden before them, and behind them a desolate wilderness; surely nothing shall escape them. Their appearance is like the appearance of horses; and like swift steeds, so they run. With a noise like chariots over mountaintops they leap, like the noise of a flaming fire that devours the stubble, like a strong people set in battle array. Before them the people writhe in pain; all faces are drained of color.* **They run like mighty men, they climb the wall like men of war; everyone marches in formation, and they do not break ranks. They do not push one another; everyone marches in his own column.** *Though they lunge between the weapons, they are not cut down. They run to and fro in the city, they run on the wall; they climb into the houses, they enter at the windows like a thief. The earth quakes before them, the heavens tremble; the sun and moon grow dark, and the stars diminish their brightness. The Lord gives voice before His army, for His camp is very great; for strong is the One who executes His word. For the day of the Lord is great and very terrible; who can endure it?* (***Joel 2:1-11 NKJV***).

This passage shows the discipline required for a fishing crew to be effective in evangelism. It is made up of people that know their place. They are good at what they do. They are resilient. They are determined to achieve their stated goals. They are not concerned about self-preservation, instead, their focus is to achieve the goals God has given to the team.

Hunting

The other way seed sown is hunting. It is when you are sowing the seeds of the gospel alone, i.e. not in partnership with other believers. A skilled sower must be able to pursue unbelievers one-on-one. A hunter usually operates alone when targeting his/her prey. A hunter is versatile and flexible in his quest to capture his prey.

Jesus Christ operated both as a fisherman and hunter during His earthly ministry. He targeted the Samaritan woman in **John 4**. He was alone and single-handedly preached the gospel to her. We also see in that same passage that the Samaritan woman went into the City as a hunter to win souls to Jesus Christ.

Many believers are more comfortable when evangelizing as part of a group. While this is an acceptable way to evangelize, we must make sure that we are also able to preach to unbelievers individually.

Just like fishing, a hunter must also have certain characteristics in order to be successful. These include patience, knowledge of the terrain and prey, endurance, flexibility and diligence.

PATIENCE
It is not unusual to see a deer hunter crouch quietly in an

inconspicuous place, waiting for the perfect opportunity to strike. The same goes for anyone who wants to evangelize, utilizing hunting techniques.

You have to be willing to wait for as long as it would take to present the gospel to the unbeliever. If the hunter hastily delivers the gospel message to the unbeliever, it can hamper, or potentially ruin the possibility of the unbeliever ever responding to the gospel.

KNOWLEDGE OF THE TERRAIN AND PREY

A good hunter must be knowledgeable of his prey and the terrain the prey operates in. In choosing who will be sent to certain individuals, God usually chooses those who are well aware of the terrain that the unbeliever operates in. God demonstrated the importance of this in sending Apostle Paul to the Gentiles, while He sent Apostle Peter to the Jews.

God can send a person to his tribe. He can send an academician to fellow scholars. He can send a mathematician to fellow mathematicians. He can send a medical practitioner to fellow medical practitioners.

ENDURANCE

A good hunter must have endurance. Because of the nature of hunting, it can take a significantly longer time to catch his/her prey, as opposed to a fishing crew catching fish.

FLEXIBILITY

A hunter is very flexible. We see in **Jeremiah 16:16 NKJV**, *"And afterward I will send for many hunters, and they* *shall hunt them from every mountain and every hill, and out of the holes of the rocks."* The hunter must be able to hunt prey in places where a fisherman's boat cannot access and egress.

DILIGENCE

Finally, a good hunter must be diligent. The bible says, *"The lazy man does not roast what he took in hunting, but diligence is man's precious possession."* (**Proverbs 12:27 NKJV**). Therefore, a good hunter promptly roasts the prey he catches in hunting. He knows that the prey he catches can start to rot if it is not promptly roasted. Roasting of prey is to a hunter, what following up with a new convert is to a skilled sower. A skilled sower must ensure that they follow up with their new converts.

Have you ever seen a lion kill prey and then walk away from the prey? Even in the animal kingdom, they understand that if they do not take away their prey, another animal will do so, or the prey will begin to rot.

A new convert that is abandoned, i.e. not followed up, is very vulnerable to the enemy's assault. The most critical time for a new believer in the first few days after they have given their life to Jesus Christ. Follow up with your new converts immediately, and ensure they know the next steps to take, now that they are born again.

To sharpen our understanding of what comes next after salvation, please read *"Now that you are born again, what next?" by Emmanuel Adewusi.*

Planting and Watering

*I planted, Apollos watered, but God gave the increase. (**1 Corinthians 3:6 NKJV**).*

Another noteworthy type of evangelism is planting and watering. In the scripture above, we noticed Paul, alluding to these types of evangelism. Just like fishing and hunting, in actual fact, we are expected to be ready for God's use as He deems fit.

PLANTING

Just like Paul, the Apostle, this is when God uses us to plant the seed of the words through talks or deeds into another individual or body. In **1 Corinthians 4:15 NLT**: *For even if you had ten thousand others to teach you about Christ, you have only one spiritual father. For I became your father in Christ Jesus when I preached the Good News to you.* Paul alluded to the fact that He planted the seed in Corinth by preaching/talking to them. Therefore, each and every time we target, share and portray the Word of God with an individual or a group of people, we are planting a seed. The Bible made us understand from **Matthew 13** that the Word of God is the seed. Each and every time it is shared and portrayed; it will fall on different kinds of ground.

Because of the nature of planting, people's hearts represent the ground. This means that we have to go after them with proper strategy. Therefore, planting is synonymous with hunting and every characteristic of hunting applies.

WATERING

Watering is simply an after-care process that comes after planting. This is synonymous to what we discussed about diligence in hunting. In this process, a seed has been planted, preservation and caring are needed to ensure the seed grows. As established earlier, the seed is the word, therefore, anything that will enhance the growth and preservation of the seed is watering.

The growth of the seed depends on this after-care. The watering process is therefore extremely important. So, choosing who to do this is solely the work of the Holy Spirit. However, we are still needed. Just as God through the Holy Spirit, identifies who and how to hunt, fish and where to plant, He also strategically puts us in places that need watering.

Sometimes, the Holy Spirit might allow the same person who planted, to water. But from **1 Corinthians 3:6**, we see in this case that it was another that watered. This is a possibility as the choice of who plants and water especially are that of the Holy Spirit.

There are two ways to plant and to water that I will highlight here. These are talking and observation.

Talking

Many times, seeds are planted by talking. When this seed is planted, the individual may not be convinced. They may have questions(s) and need help making that last jump. In some cases, they can ask the planter, but often time, they might not have that opportunity. But if they know us to be Christians, they may approach us and ask. This, therefore, gives room for the watering process through talks.

During this period, we can share our experiences and testimonies as led by the Holy Spirit. We can invite them to Church and help them get rooted. We must be diligent to seek answers to their question(s) even if we don't know it at the point. Once they become saved, they have become our brethren in Christ who we can help grow until they become an "adult" in God. This is a watering process through talks.

Observation

Observation is another significant and common unknowing planting and watering process. There are people that will never read the Bible or go to any Christian gathering. But guess what? They are watching and observing us. They may have said in their hearts, "he says he is a Christian, let's see if he'll compromise". They may have heard this evangelism record before (that is, the initial seed may have been planted), but they are not convinced. Others are just curious as to the fact that who is a Christian? Or is there a God? But they will never ask because they judge by observation. So, they lay in wait observing us.

Some of these people are located strategically around us. Some at our workplaces, sports teams and several other places. These people believe in actions rather than our words. Therefore, living a holy life is not just for us to make heaven, but it is also so that the Holy Spirit, who convicts, can use our life to water and plant as needed. When the scripture commands us in **1 Corinthians 10:31 NLT** that *whether you eat or drink, or whatever you do, do it all for the glory of God.* This is one of the reasons.

However, even though we should do a form of these types of evangelism every day in our daily life, it does not replace the leading of the Holy Spirit on what type of evangelism to employ. Whatever strategy God wants, that is exactly what we must do. We might not know who we may have watered or the seed we have planted through observation. But God knows. So, we must always let God lead the way.

Let God Lead the Way

Many people receive "marching orders" from God to complete an assignment, and they run off on their own to do it, without allowing God to lead the way. It seems like many people are trying to say to God, "All I need from you is where you want me to go. Once I get the vision, I can find my way there on my own". This doesn't make good sense. We must remain in a position where we are being led by God.

Many believers have believed the lie that, so long as they are doing something good, they are pleasing God. This is absolutely false. Remember that Jesus Himself said, *"Not everyone that saith unto me, Lord, Lord, shall enter into the kingdom of heaven; but he that doeth the will of my Father which is in heaven. Many will say to me in that day, Lord, Lord, have we not prophesied in thy name? and in thy name have cast out devils? and in thy name done many wonderful works? And then will I profess unto them, I never knew you: depart from me, ye that work iniquity"*

(**Matthew 7:21-23 KJV**). The word of God also says, *"For as many as are led by the Spirit of God, they are the sons of God"* (**Romans 8:14 NKJV**). Do not fall for this misconception. Acting on God's behalf, without being expressly commissioned by God to do so, is a misrepresentation. It is wrong and improper. God has commissioned us all to preach the gospel, but He still holds the prerogative to assign different believers to different tasks and harvest fields. You are susceptible to the trap of the devil if you keep doing whatever you feel like doing for God, without God's permission.

Even though God desires everyone to be eventually saved (See **1 Timothy 2:4**), there is a time and season appointed by God for that to take place. Salvation is indeed appointed. An appointment means that there is a schedule. It is written in **Acts 13:48 NKJV**, *"Now when the Gentiles heard this, they were glad and glorified the word of the Lord. And as many as had been appointed to eternal life believed."* This means that if we are not careful, we might be ministering to people that God has not appointed to be saved yet.

We are not to evangelize based on emotions, human strategy, or our own understanding. Allow God to direct your soul-winning endeavors. In soul winning, there is both the human planning side and the aspect where the Holy Spirit leads. Both work in tandem. Whenever there is self-seeking or a selfish agenda on the part of the soul-winner, it will become difficult, if not impossible for them to be led by the Holy Spirit.

FORBIDDEN TO PREACH THE WORD IN ASIA

There is an interesting account in **Acts 16:6-10 NKJV** that is worthy of analysis.

Now when they had gone through Phrygia and the region of Galatia, they were forbidden by the Holy Spirit to preach the word in Asia. After they had come to Mysia, they tried to go into Bithynia, but the Spirit did not permit them. So, passing by Mysia, they came down to Troas. And a vision appeared to Paul in the night. A man of Macedonia stood and pleaded with him, saying, "Come over to Macedonia and help us." Now after he had seen the vision, immediately we sought to go to Macedonia, concluding that the Lord had called us to preach the gospel to them.

Paul and Silas were travelling westward through a territory known in the Bible as Asia. The places they visited are now in the country of modern-day Turkey. In chapter 16 verse 6, the writer of the Book of Acts says, *"They passed through the Phrygian and Galatian region, having been forbidden by the Holy Spirit to speak the word in Asia."* Here, we see the Holy Spirit at work in changing the plans of Paul and Silas.

When Luke says that the Spirit had forbidden Paul to speak the Word in Asia, he implies that Paul wanted to do so. No doubt, at some point, Paul had made his desire known to his missionary team. Although Luke does not mention Ephesus, the chief city of Asia, it is likely that Paul wanted to proclaim the gospel there. Ephesus was a great commercial, religious, and cultural center. However, the Holy Spirit postponed Paul's preaching there. In God's time, Paul went to Ephesus for ministry. He went there, near the end of his second missionary journey (See **Acts 18:19-21**), and returned on his third journey.

After Paul and Silas arrived in Mysia, in the northwest of modern Turkey, they wanted to turn north into the northern province of Bithynia. Apparently, they had a strategy they wanted to implement. The northern part of Bithynia was on the southern coast of the Black Sea. A key city in this northern province was Nicea. This would be a great place to take the gospel.

Now, for a second time, the Holy Spirit intervened. The Holy Spirit did not permit the missionary team to go to Bithynia. This was a historic moment in the history of the church. The Holy Spirit turned the attention of Paul and his team to Europe instead of Bithynia. Throughout the Book of Acts, the pivotal moments are described as coming from the Spirit. God's strategy for world evangelism was Europe before Asia.

Within fifteen years, Peter finally took the gospel to Bithynia, according to the salutation of his first epistle (See **1 Peter 1:1**).

LED BY THE HOLY SPIRIT TO MACEDONIA

When the Holy Spirit leads, we know we are acting in accordance with God's time and purpose. Very often, we may wish to do very good things, but it is not God's time. He alone is the master of all things. He alone knows when to act. He alone knows the circumstances that prevail at any given time. Because of this, we can have full confidence in the guidance of the Spirit.

God speaks and leads us in a variety of ways. Sometimes God reveals His will through a vision. God spoke to Ananias (See **Acts 9:10-12**) in a vision about Paul and his ministry. The Lord spoke to Cornelius (See **Acts 10:3**) and Peter (See **Acts 10:17-19**; **Acts 11:5**) in visions. These visions led to the breakthrough of the gospel among the Gentiles.

At Troas, on the northwestern coast of modern Turkey, the Lord spoke to Paul through a vision (See **Acts 16:9**). In the vision, a man from Macedonia was standing and appealing to Paul to come to Macedonia. This was a powerful and persuasive way for Paul to be called. God not only prevented Paul and his team from preaching in Asia and going to Bithynia, but also gave them a positive direction on what to do. He called them to Macedonia, which is a part of Europe.

The missionary team (fishing crew) did not hesitate to respond to the call. Luke (**Acts 16:10**) says, *"Immediately we sought to go into Macedonia, concluding that God had called us to preach the gospel to them."*

What a striking story! Twice in this short story, Paul and his team were supernaturally led by the Holy Spirit. Then, Paul had his vision of the man from Macedonia. All this kept Paul in harmony with God's plan to keep going through Asia and on to Europe. We can sum all this up with **Proverbs 16:9 NKJV**. *It says, "The mind of man plans his way, But the Lord directs his steps."* As we commit ourselves to the Lord, we know that He will lead us day by day. God's strategy must prevail.

Without the active leading of the Holy Spirit, our well-intentioned soul-winning endeavors will be a waste. If you continue regardless, you will risk falling into the trap of satisfying yourself, which will eventually lead to pride.

There is time for everything and God is in control of the times and seasons. According to **Ecclesiastes 3:1-2 NKJV**, *"To everything there is a season, a time for every purpose under heaven: A time to be born, and a time to die; a time to plant, and a time to pluck what is planted."*

Whenever we are not in alignment with God's will, the devil will have a field day stealing from us (See **John 10:10**). We are most secure when we are in God's perfect will. The most effective way to remain in command and be fruitful is to be fully under God's authority. When we are aligned to God's will, it is impossible for the devil to take advantage of us, except if it was ordained by God to further His plan. For example, the devil believed he was destroying the ministry of Jesus Christ when he moved the people to crucify Him but never knew that the death of Jesus Christ on the cross was part of God's plan for redeeming mankind (See **1 Corinthians 2:8**). Another example is in the life of Job. Scripture records that Job's latter end was more blessed than his beginning (See **Job 42:12**).

4

The Hurdle and How to Overcome

For every promise of God, there is a blessing that comes with it (See **Deuteronomy 28**). These blessings get us closer to God, increase our faith in Him, and make it increasingly hard for the devil to win us over. Also, everything God wants us to do will favor God's cause on earth, and most importantly us (hence the blessing). Therefore, the devil will always suffer a loss every time we obey God. Take evangelism, for example, the moment we step into action, we are on the verge of potentially winning soul(s) for God and de-populate hell in the process. Keep in mind, however, that we cannot evangelize unless we are saved first. This means that we are saved and obeying God, so we are a lost cause for the devil. We are creating havoc by spreading the knowledge of Jesus, which will potentially get another person(s) into the kingdom of God. From our individual and overall standpoint, this is a loss for the devil and he will not take such lightly.

Since every command of God creates a loss for the devil,

he came up with a simple yet effective way, a long time ago, to defeat us and keep us from obeying God. This way produces different effects as needed to mitigate his loss. So, we can call this way a tool that can be used in different forms to produce the desired results. The devil deploys this tool strategically as needed for each application. A closer analysis at each end result will reveal that the devil only has one tool of operation.

The devil realizes that losses only come when Christians (children of God) step into the place of authority and take actions as commanded. He is well aware that the right action can only be sustained by true understanding. There is no such thing as luck in spirituality; it is impossible to continually take the right action without the right understanding. Due to this fact, the devil hinders Christians from getting the right understanding, where it is needed (hence the reason for the advice in **Proverbs 4:7**).

We must understand that our nature is a curious nature. It is always longing for information to process. Understanding is the result of processed information. Whatever we understand about anything or anyone, is because of how the information received was processed. The devil is also known as Satan knowing that this nature of ours cannot be left empty then feeds us with his own fabricated truth. I call this fabricated truth because not all information designed to deceive are lies, some are just half-truth and half lie; it is whatever can make us gullible enough to fall for it. This process is known as deception.

"You won't die!" the serpent replied to the woman. "God knows

*that your eyes will be opened as soon as you eat it, and you will be like God, knowing both good and evil." (**Genesis 3:4-5 NLT**)*

The information given to Eve in the scripture above is an example of fabricated truth. The devil solely designed this information to make Eve disobey God. It was true that once Eve and Adam ate the fruit their eyes would be open, and they would know both good and evil. But this is deception because it omits the key detail of destruction that comes with that knowledge. Instead, he portrayed the fact that they would be smart enough to survive independent of God. Information fed through deception is then used as a weapon to aid the restriction fences and hurdles such as fear in the case of evangelism.

Therefore, the tool is deception, and the effect it produces on us, which in the case of evangelism is fear.

The focus of this chapter is to identify and understand this devilish approach and how to overcome it.

*so that Satan will not outsmart us. For we are familiar with his evil schemes. (**2 Corinthians 2:11 NLT**)*

Once we know and understand the strategy, we can easily overcome the devil with the help of God. As explained in the "the necessity of understanding" section in the introduction, our understanding is essential to our standing with God. Therefore, our understanding determines our standing with God.

Arguments

Before we get into fear, I will highlight a very common

trick the devil uses that most of us often fall into. Just like every other thing, when the devil realizes that he couldn't get us to back down, he then goes the extra mile to make sure that we are not productive. And thereby defeating the purpose and robbing us of our blessings/rewards. Yes, God has made evangelism a thing for all Christian—mature and baby; however, it is still in our purview to understand a few things that are not acceptable. Arguments are one of those things we can never get engaged in.

The Holy Spirit is the one who convicts. It is His job to prove Himself, not ours. Arguing is trying to do the job of the Holy Spirit. We are not there to prove but to convey the message of God's saving grace.

*And when he comes, he will convict the world of its sin, and of God's righteousness, and of the coming judgment. (**John 16:8 NLT**)*

Our job is to say the word and the other person listens. Argument contradicts this command therefore it is not allowed. As mentioned earlier, when we argue, we are doing the work of the Holy Spirit and as such He will step aside. When this happens, we become a vulnerable and defeat-able target. In fact, going to evangelize without the Holy Spirit is like going into the lion's den. Truth is, there are many deceptive and confident wolves out there, some with a sound intellectual mind and others with a demonic mind and power. I am not saying this to scare us, but to let us understand that it is the protection of the Holy Spirit that can keep the wolves contained. And we stand no chance without Him. Therefore, any argument during evangelism stands a great chance of pushing us in this dangerous direction.

But you may say well, what if a question arises when talking to a person of another faith. Are you saying not to answer questions? Absolutely not. I am an advocate for asking questions; there is no true understanding without asking the right questions. However, we must understand that there is a distinct difference between an argument and asking a genuine question.

The argument is presenting your view for the sake of convincing others; thereby winning the contest. As we all know, it takes great sportsmanship to end a contest without dislike/hatred or violence, which is another reason argument cannot have a place in evangelism.

A person who asks a genuine question wants an answer, and therefore will listen. They want to know; so, they ask. Such a person possesses a positive attitude and a teachable spirit; therefore, he/she requires our full attention and explanation.

On the other hand, when an argumentative person asks a question, they ask not to listen but to create a platform for them to present their view and argue to win. Once we notice this, we should just politely leave them be. Such a person is not ready to listen, maybe they are not ripe for harvest yet. So, they will waste our time and their time. In fact, in the case of a baby Christian, we could do more damage to ourselves just by listening to them. Beware.

*If any household or town refuses to welcome you or listen to your message, shake its dust from your feet as you leave. (**Matthew 10:14 NLT**)*

The Hurdle: Fear

One of the major obstacles and hindrances in Christianity is Fear. It is important to know that the main reason for fear is to delay, obstruct and disrupt God's work here on earth. As faith is needed to bring God into action, fear is needed to stop God from acting. Therefore, fear is of the devil. Fear is one of the most important, dependable, and effective lieutenants of the devil. In the kingdom of darkness, fear is the go-to to get things done. This means that fear is a spirit and as such, it can possess, oppress, and control. In the realm of the spirit, lieutenants of the devil are referred to as demons.

*For God has not given us a spirit of fear, but of power and of love and of a sound mind. (**2 Timothy 1:7 NLT**)*

Being a Christian does not restrict the influence of demons on us. When we became born-again Christians, our Spirit received the regenerative power of God. Our spirit connects with the Holy Spirit to affirm our relationship with God. Therefore, at the beginning of our relationship with God, the starting point is our spirit and then (if allowed) it spreads to the other parts of our being—soul and body.

*For his Spirit joins with our spirit to affirm that we are God's children. (**Romans 8:16 NLT**).*

Once we receive the Holy Spirit, our spirit is connected but our soul and body are still what they used to be. This is the reason for the conflicts we sometimes experience between the body, soul, and spirit after salvation.

The sinful nature wants to do evil, which is just the opposite of what the Spirit wants. And the Spirit gives us desires that are the opposite of what the sinful nature desires. These two forces are con-

*stantly fighting each other, so you are not free to carry out your good intentions. (**Galatians 5:17 NLT**).*

*I don't really understand myself, for I want to do what is right, but I don't do it. Instead, I do what I hate. (**Romans 7:15 NLT**)*

Every good thing that is destined for us to exhibit as Christians is already available in our spirit the moment we are saved. But this can only become visible after what is in our spirit is somehow reproduced in our soul and body. Many Christians find it hard to implement our spirit (which is now connected with the Holy Spirit) commands like Apostle Paul in **Romans 7:15**; this is because there is no link between the spirit and the body yet. At this point, you are probably thinking but how do I ensure my body does what is pleasing to the Spirit? The answer is to *let the Holy Spirit (through your regenerated spirit) guide your lives. Then you won't be doing what your sinful nature craves* (**Galatians 5:16 NLT**, emphasis added*); and those who are dominated by the sinful nature think about sinful things, but those who are controlled by the Holy Spirit think about things that please the Spirit.* (**Romans 8:5 NLT**). Yes, we exist in the physical realm—our body, but it is our responsibility to obey the Spirit rather than our bodily cravings. We must be mindful of the Spirit. The more we do this, the easier it becomes to bring our body and soul under the subjection of the Spirit. I am not suggesting that this is going to be a walk in the park, however, if God has set up a system like this then it simply means that He has given us the ability to do it (See **Deuteronomy 30:11**). Which means, we can do it. To learn more about the Holy Spirit and How to engage Him, I encourage you to read *"The Most Important Person of Our Time" by Ebenezer Agboola and "The Holy Spirit: An Introduction" by John Bevere.*

The temptations in your life are no different from what others experience. And God is faithful. He will not allow the temptation to be more than you can stand. When you are tempted, he will show you a way out so that you can endure. (**1 Corinthians 10:13 NLT**).

The engagement of our spirit in everything we do gives access to the Holy Spirit to do the regenerative work in the other parts of our being. You hear Christians say things like "I don't desire that anymore." This kind of thing only happens after we have given the Holy Spirit access to renew our soul and body. This is exactly what Apostle Paul meant by the instruction he gave below.

And so, dear brothers and sisters, I plead with you to give your bodies to God (the Holy Spirit) because of all he has done for you. Let them be a living and holy sacrifice—the kind he will find acceptable. This is truly the way to worship him. Don't copy the behavior and customs of this world but let God (the Holy Spirit) transform you into a new person by changing the way you think (your mind—soul). Then you will learn to know God's (the Holy Spirit's) will for you, which is good and pleasing and perfect. (**Romans 12:1-2 NLT, emphasis added**)

We are a new creation (See **2 Corinthians 5:17**). Yes, as Christians, we cannot be possessed by anything else other than the Spirit of God. But it is still possible to be oppressed or influenced by demons. As established earlier, when we became born-again, our spirit is regenerated and reborn. However, our soul and body only follow suit after we've given access to the Holy Spirit. The regeneration and transformation of the body and soul happen over a period of time, the speed of this reaction is solely based on the individual and the amount of access given to the Spirit of God. However, it must be noted that because we are in the body and are exposed to negative things daily, this process is therefore a continuous work of the Holy Spirit for the rest of our days. This work of the Holy Spirit is known as sanctification. Remember, He is a Gentleman and will never force His way beyond what's given. He connects with our spirit only after we have received Jesus, and ask for Him (See **Luke 11:13**).

*And if anyone does not have the Spirit of Christ (Holy Spirit), he does not belong to Jesus Christ. (**Romans 8:9b NLT**, emphasis added)*

So, to get Him into our other beings, permission is needed. Our soul and body remain what they were before we became saved unless we allow this regeneration. We must learn to renew our mind continually after we become saved thus the need for sanctification. From this fact, we can deduce that our mind and body are still open to the oppression of the demons, but our spirit is a no-go area for demons. Therefore, even after salvation, you can still feel those desires you felt before salvation.

Spirits connect with spirits and influence other beings from there. For demons, once we carelessly allow them to enter our spirit, they can take charge of the remaining being by force. The devil and his demons are not gentle but are slave masters. They do not respect the human's free will. This is called possession. Therefore, a demon-possessed person acts erratically in the body according to the wish of the demon rather than that of the person. The Spirit of God on the other hand only influences our other parts when given Him that chance. Otherwise, He will remain in our spirit. God gave us free will and His Spirit respects our desires. He is not a dictator like demons but seeks our permission to turn our life around for good.

*"Look! I stand at the door and knock. If you hear my voice and open the door, I will come in, and we will share a meal together as friends. (**Revelation 3:20 NLT**)*

Now that we have discussed why some Christians are still acting in non-Christian ways. It is the same reason some of us are fearful. The simple answer is that we have given the Holy Spirit little or no access to turn our life around. This is dangerous because the Holy Spirit, like every other spirit, longs to influence all of our beings; this is one of His many purposes. Our spirit is just an entryway for Him to have access to our whole being. However, the more we ignore/confine Him into our spirit only, the more we give power to the other parts of our beings who may still be under the influence of the devil. Eventually, the higher power wins and the Holy Spirit might be kicked out of our spirit altogether. Therefore, what we obey is what we become. Our obedience to the Holy Spirit strengthens His ability, access, and our friendship with Him.

*So, letting your sinful nature control your mind leads to death. But letting the Spirit control your mind (soul) leads to life and peace. (**Roman 8:6 NLT**; emphasis added)*

*The one who sows to please his flesh, from the flesh will reap destruction; but the one who sows to please the Spirit, from the Spirit will reap eternal life. (**Galatian 6:8 NLT**)*

Therefore, as Christians, we are always advised to consult the Holy Spirit. This is because the body and the soul can easily be tricked when we don't get our regenerated spirit involved. So, the point is that the fact that you are a Christian does not make you an exception to the oppression or influence from the spirit of fear.

Fear is a major concern that must be addressed for all. Most of our negative actions and reactions are done because of fear. Low self-esteem is rooted in fear, at the core of pride is fear. Intimidations and limitations are all associates and the result of fear. The struggle of many people is based on the oppression/possession of fear.

Fear is a demon that deception opened the door for. It starts with a thought in our mind; our meditation on this thought then leads to assumptions, misconceptions and hence misinformation. The misinformation and/or misrepresentation is the deception part of this whole plan.

Due to our curiosity, our mind tends to wander. This implies that no matter our status as born-again or not, we all have thoughts that pop in and out of our minds, every now and then. This is one of the many strategies the devil uses (the act of suggestion) to gain access to us. How does the devil do this? Having a thought does not make us a sinner. It only shows our human nature. The world we live in today is filled with many things. And as such we can see, hear and experience different things. Most of our thoughts are therefore often brewed from all that we are exposed to. Our nature comes up with so many thoughts, some of which are baseless, useless and will later disappear unless we decide to meditate on any of them. This is what makes us human; our ability to choose what we meditate on. Meditation can be deemed as a form of agreeing with a certain thought.

Guard your heart (thoughts) above all else, for it determines the course of your life. Avoid all perverse talk; stay away from corrupt speech. Look, straight ahead, and fix your eyes on what lies before you. Mark, out a straight path for your feet; stay on the safe path. Don't get sidetracked; keep your feet from following evil. (**Proverbs 4:23-27 NLT; emphasis added**)

The scripture above is complete. It makes us understand that what we meditate on determines our actions. And our actions shape our lives. It also goes on and describes how to guard our thoughts.

Just like the popular saying, "prevention is better than cure." The Bible is telling us that when it comes to what we expose ourselves to, it is better not to be exposed to certain things than fighting the thoughts later.

This is important because it is one of the many ways the devil deceives us. Many of us will never think or imagine certain things if not for what we are exposed to. Fear, like every other agent of the devil, starts from here.

For better understanding, let's look at a man named Marco. He's got a great idea to start a great business. He decided to pursue this idea and set out to seek information on what he is trying to do. However, in this quest, he told Muffy about his great idea. But Muffy's experiences with business in the past were not great. So, Muffy shared his opinion and certain things to consider. Marco went home and couldn't get Muffy's negativity out of his head. This was the end of the "great idea". What just happened? Well, fear kills. And that was what happened in the case of Marco. Muffy might have shared those experiences out of honesty, but it was Marco who set himself up for that information; hence be watchful of whom you seek advice from. That information would have remained in Muffy if Marco didn't search for it. Muffy's words started a thought, Marco meditated on that thought and gave room to the spirit of fear. This eventually pushed him to make a decision that determined the course of his life.

Thoughts are bound to disappear after a few minutes of inaction. When you meditate on something it stays and becomes part of you. The moment this happens, you have opened the door to either God or the devil. Truth is when you meditate, you are in search of information to satisfy your quest(ion); everything about your being (spirit, soul, and body) is searching and open to get an answer(s). Therefore, meditation is a way to connect with the spirit realm. When you meditate, you are open spiritually. As Christians, we meditate on the word/ways/acts of God, ask Him for answers in prayer and spend time with the Holy Spirit. This is done to ensure that we are open to the right side of the spiritual. Every other form of meditation has the tendency of getting us connected to the wrong side which may land us in trouble. The Holy Spirit helps us to navigate the realm of the spirit. It is through meditation that the Holy Spirit often has access to us (See **Acts 10:19**). This is because our spirit is open, it is therefore easy for the Holy Spirit to give us answers and flow into our being. In these moments of meditation, we are vulnerable, hungry, and desperate for answers. When meditation is not done with God as stated earlier, all kinds of evil spirits (fear included), seeking an opportunity to possess, oppress, influence are alerted.

God blesses those who hunger and thirst for justice, for they will be satisfied. (**Matthew 5:6 NLT**)

No one can know a person's thoughts except that person's own spirit, and no one can know God's thoughts except God's own Spirit. (**1 Corinthians 2:11 NLT**)

So, we noticed that the same way God gets His Spirit into our being and gives us answers, the devil also uses this avenue to give us lies and get access for his demons, in this case, the spirit of fear into our being.

Once, fear is in through deception, the spirit will seek to control all our beings. Therefore, if possible, it may seek to occupy our most sacred place, our spirit. But as Christians, because we are born again and are baptized in the Holy Spirit, we have the Spirit of God in us. Therefore, He is the current occupant of our spirit.

Don't you realize that all of you together are the temple of God and that the Spirit of God lives in you? (1 Corinthians 3:16 NLT)

Instead of fighting the Holy Spirit in our spirit (an already lost battle), fear sticks with either our soul and/or body. It oppresses and influences our body and soul; subject either or both of these two under its control, even though our spirit may want something else. If as Christian, we still have the Spirit of God in our spirit, we can occasionally snap out of the control of fear and act according to the Spirit. But not until we allow the sanctification process, the second regenerative work of the Holy Spirit after salvation. Which puts us completely under the Holy Spirit; this work purifies us from (our spirit, to our soul and finally it is revealed in the body) the inside out. Any of us can still be poked by the spirit of fear. As I mentioned before, when you are oppressed, and you always succumb to the desire of your soul and/or body, as a child of God, it simply means you are not in control and have lost access to the Holy Spirit at that point in time. This becomes uncomfortable for and brings sorrow to the Holy Spirit. And if this continues unchecked, it is possible to lose the Holy Spirit in the process.

"No one can serve two masters. For you will hate one and love the other; you will be devoted to one and despise the other. You cannot serve both God and money (fear). (**Matthew 6:24 NLT, emphasis added**)

And do not bring sorrow to God's Holy Spirit by the way you live. Remember, he has identified you as his own, guaranteeing that you will be saved on the day of redemption. (**Ephesians 4:30 NLT**)

Now, with fear's access to the body and/or soul, this demon will then start to oppress and influence. The deception continues; until we confront this issue with the help of the Holy Spirit, God's word and prayer, it never stops until we fail and fall (See **John 10:10**). This becomes even easier when a portion of us is under the control of this demon. Intimidations, low self-esteem and much more negativity set in. We can now think of many reasons we should not/cannot or are not qualified to evangelize. Irrelevant things become relevant and we end up disobeying God. This is the same process used by the devil all the time. This is his only tool to get us to sin, we must know and be familiar with it. For the sake of explanation, let's assume that the deception of Eve in the garden of Eden was thought that the devil drops in her heart, we will see a striking similarity in the devilish deceptive style. Whether the devil does it in person or through our thoughts, he uses the same strategy. Read the account below.

One day he asked the woman, "Did God really say you must not eat the fruit from any of the trees in the garden?" (Assumed: this was a thought in Eve's mind) "Of course, we may eat fruit from the trees in the garden," the woman replied. "It's only the fruit from the tree in the middle of the garden that we are not allowed to eat. God said, 'You must not eat it or even touch it; if you do, you will die.'" (Assumed: this was her response during meditations). "You won't die!" the serpent replied to the woman (Deception begins). "God knows that your eyes will be opened as soon as you eat it, and you will be like God, knowing both good and evil (True, but not completely true... (Deception continues))." The woman was convinced (The spirit of disobedient steps in). She saw that the tree was beautiful, and its fruit looked delicious, and she wanted the wisdom it would give her. So, she took some of the fruit and ate it (Actions that shape the course of life-Proverbs 4:23). Then she gave some to her husband, who was with her, and he ate it, too (Action continues). At that moment their eyes were opened, and they suddenly felt shame at their nakedness. So, they sewed fig leaves together to cover *themselves (Consequences of disobedient-sin). (**Genesis 3:1-7 NLT, emphasis added**)*

Another side of the coin is the bondage of fear. For Christians, being oppressed and/or influenced simply means some parts (soul and/or body) are tied up with that hostile demon. But one can lose all parts if proper care is not taken. Bondage by fear is a bit different; it means being possessed by the spirit of fear. This often occurs only to unbelievers; when this happens, they cannot move forward at all. The spirit of fear dictates everything. The Holy Spirit is the gentle Spirit, demons are not. Therefore, when demons take over the spirit of a person, the desires of the person become irrelevant. The absolute control belongs to the spirit they are possessed by (see **Mark 5** and **Luke 8:26-39**). The only path to freedom for such a person is to receive Jesus otherwise they are doomed.

Now that we understand that fear is a demon sent to hinder us from doing the will of God, in this case, evangelism, how do we then overcome fear?

The Solution: Love

*Such love has no fear, because perfect love expels all fear. If we are afraid, it is for fear of punishment, and this shows that we have not fully experienced his perfect love. (**1 John 4:18 NLT**)*

Love, an interesting word that has been used in many different ways (most of which are wrong) in our time. Many have been hurt because of this word. Today, there are so many meanings given to love. But there is only one true meaning to love and that is our focus here. Every other kind that does not fall within the definition given in this book will not be considered. Ideally, all love should be modelled after God's kind of love. So, what is God's kind of love? To really understand what that is we need to know how God loves. Once this is defined, then we can break it down and see how this kind of love will help us overcome fear.

GOD'S KIND OF LOVE

The God kind of love is God. This is a simple yet profound definition of love. *But anyone who does not love does not know God, for God is love.* (**1 John 4:8 NLT**)

You might be thinking this doesn't make sense, how can God be love? God does not have love, He is love. The same way in the body, I am a man, in relating with us, God is love. This is who He is. For lack of a better word, love is the essence of God. Therefore, He is so merciful and gracious. To prove this point let us look at the parable Jesus gave to define God's kind of love.

*So, Jesus told them this story: "If a man has a hundred sheep and one of them gets lost, what will he do? Won't he leave the ninety-nine others in the wilderness and go to search for the one that is lost until he finds it? And when he has found it, he will joyfully carry it home on his shoulders. When he arrives, he will call together his friends and neighbors, saying, 'Rejoice with me because I have found my lost sheep.' In the same way, there is more joy in heaven over one lost sinner who repents and returns to God than over ninety-nine others who are righteous and haven't strayed away! (**Luke 15:3-7 NLT**)*

Not many people will leave ninety-nine sheep for just one. But with God, it's a different story. His love is unfathomable. He cannot help Himself but save humanity. He loves us so much that He was and is still willing to go the extra mile. He laid His life for us. This is the God kind of love; it is the nature of God and therefore unnatural for us. Therefore, this kind of love is the fruit we produce only through the Holy Spirit.

*There is no greater love than to lay down one's life for one's friends. (**John 15:13 NLT**)*

Every act of God is done out of love. The acts of God are therefore the reflection of the love of God. But what about those acts in the Old Testament? If we can understand and see things from God's perspective with the help of the Holy Spirit, we'll realize that even those acts are out of love. The God kind of love is God and to learn about this love, we must know God and His acts (See **1 Corinthians 13**). But how does God's kind of love help us overcome fear?

Love and Fear

Jesus replied, '"You must love the LORD your God with all your heart, all your soul, and all your mind.' This is the first and greatest commandment. And the second is like it: 'Love your neighbor as yourself.' (***Matthew 22:37-39 NLT***)

The scripture above reveals to us the only law that matters in the new testament (our time). However, this love is a triangle with three sides that God requires from us. Our love towards God, ourselves and our neighbor are the three sides of this love. It must be noted that our neighbor is anyone we are able to help when they are in need (see **Luke 10**). These three sides of the love triangle have their own distinct character that eliminates and get rid of fear. Every characteristic of love is the opposite of fear and has the capacity to overcome fear or render it powerless. In this section, we will learn a few of many of these characteristics.

1. Love is of God and Fear is of the devil: As established earlier, God is love; and as such, His acts, nature and who He is, exhibit love. Fear is of the devil and he uses this on us to destroy and ruin the plan of God. So, for a fact, we know that because fear is of the devil then there is no fear in God; and no love in the devil. God is not fearful, so, if we live fully in God—love (through holiness life) and we are His children, then we cannot be fearful or live in fear. Therefore, if God has commanded us to evangelize, then the fear we feel only reveals that we are paying attention to the devil rather than the one who has sent us.

*Such love has no fear, because perfect love expels all fear. If we are afraid, it is for fear of punishment, and this shows that we have not fully experienced his perfect love. (**1 John 4:18 NLT**)*

*For God has not given us a spirit of fear and timidity, but of power, love, and self-discipline. (**2 Timothy 1:7 NLT**)*

2. Love portrays positivity while Fear feeds on negativity: Love does not believe or see the worst in us and others. Therefore, it is impossible to be in love and do wrong to our neighbor. This makes it impossible for fear to operate. Fear needs and germinates in the negatives which means seeing the wrong in people and ourselves. And keeping records of those wrongs. Remember, the spirit of fear gains access through deception (which is lies and/or half-truths). The God kind of love eliminates all these by giving us the right perspectives, making it the opposite and enemy of fear.

Love does no wrong to others, so love fulfills the requirements of God's law. (**Romans 13:10 NLT**).

Love does not demand its own way. It is not irritable, and it keeps no record of being wronged. (**1 Corinthians 13:5 NLT**)

3. Faith, the opposite of fear: Fear says:" what if", and faith says:" what if not." Fear says: you cannot do it; Faith says: yes, you can do it. So, we see that faith is the clear opposite of fear. But what is the relationship between faith and love? Faith only works through love. But how? Our love for God increases our faith in Him. Our love draws us closer making it possible to know Him more and hence increase trust which leads to faith. Therefore, our love for God enhances our faith in Him. The closer we get to God, the more we are exposed to Him, this increases our trust and ultimately our faith. So, faith works through love.

For in Christ Jesus neither circumcision nor uncircumcision avails anything, but faith working through love. (**Galatians 5:6 NLT**)

4. Love produces compassion: If we are going to evangelize with the right intention, souls for the kingdom, then we need compassion. However, this is something impossible to have without God's kind of love towards our fellow humans. Naturally, we are prone to not wanting to act because we have been saved. But with love comes compassion, and with compassion comes soul winning. If we are going to portray a loving God, then we must do that with compassion, otherwise, no reward should be expected. Love and compassion are inseparable combos. When we have compassion, it makes it difficult for fear to operate because our compassion will make us immune to the lies of the devil that gives root to fear. All we see when we are compassionate is a person drowning and needing help. Our ability to help springs us into action, defeating the goal of fear.

When he saw the crowds, he had compassion on them because they were confused and helpless, like sheep without a shepherd. (**Matthew 9:36 NLT**)

But you, O Lord, are a God of compassion and mercy, slow to get angry and filled with unfailing love and faithfulness. (**Psalm 86:15 NLT**)

5

Conclusion

We know that the promises of God were initially meant for the Israel-nation. However, the blessing pronounced on Abraham by God revealed that He had planned to extend these blessings to all humans.

And through your descendants, all the nations of the earth will be blessed--all because you have obeyed me." (**Genesis 22:18 NLT**)

Now we understand that God was referring to Jesus when He blessed Abraham in the scripture above. All other people would have remained in bondage of sin, if not for the obedience of Abraham and the courage of his physical descendant who extended this blessing of Jesus to us all (The Apostles et.al). Jesus came as a Jew and died a Jew. In fact, during Jesus' lifetime, He did not visit other nations and/or races (except Samaritans in **John 4**). This was because His mission in those three years was to get the disciples trained for evangelism and die for our salvation.

Therefore, we see that we (the other people) cannot claim to be Christians (God's beloved), if not for evangelism. The disciples, plus Apostle Paul, obeyed God, took the steps and got us to God. Though few of the disciples objected to God's concept of saving gentile, for those that allowed God, He was able to convince them that salvation is meant for all (See **Acts 10**). If not for their obedience and courage we would have been doomed. So, a person who claims to be saved (through evangelism) but decides not to evangelize is clearly kicking against God's way of doing things.

From what is going on in the world today, we can say that the survival of our faith (both corporately and individually) may depend on evangelism. Therefore, it is important to God. Evangelism is about God not about us. Yes, sometimes we get to share our testimony; however, the moment we shift our focus away from God and to ourselves, it becomes difficult and impossible.

The only primary law from Jesus to all Christian is love (see **Matthew 22:39**). Not evangelizing literally violates this command. I would like us to go through a couple of points on how this violates our core—love.

- How can we claim to love our neighbor and not have compassion? Someone once said, "if you understand the danger of hell, you will never wish for your enemy to end up there". If you are truly saved, then you somewhat understand the danger you were saved from. It is this understanding and our love toward others that leads to compassion, and this propels us to help others—our neighbors get out of similar danger. A Christian who decides not to evangelize is like a spouse who sees their significant other in or heading towards danger and does nothing. This is a pure and absolute definition of wickedness as they come. Therefore, in my own opinion, such a person is not qualified to be a Christian because they are not. You might say why is this so significant? The command in **Matthew 22:39** is to "love our neighbor as ourselves". If we love ourselves well enough to be saved, then everyone on the face of the earth–our neighbor must be given this same kind of love towards salvation.

- Love does no wrong to others (**Romans 13:10**). This is simple and straightforward. Not evangelizing simply means that we are doing wrong to others. This is because as Christians, we know that everyone who is not saved through Jesus is on the fast lane to hell. Yet, we compromise, have lunch with them and chat with them when we know hell is looming. I am not sure if there is any greater definition of wrong than this.

In conclusion, *remember, it is sin to know what you ought to do and then not do it.* (**James 4:17 NLT**). Some of us knew about evangelism and others are just understanding it. Whichever side of the aisle we find ourselves, now we know, and it is, therefore, our obligation to do it. May God help us in Jesus' name. Amen.

Contact the Author

If you have been blessed by this book, I would like to hear from you. You can let us know how this book has impacted and influenced your life at info@eagboola.com. For more information, please visit www.eagboola.com

God Bless you.

About the Book

For every child of God, knowing the heart of our Father in heaven and doing it, is the name of the game. But how can we do what we do not understand? This is the reason for this book. In this book, with the help of the Holy Spirit, we will discover the heart of God on the most important act today. Why is it not just for some people, but for every child of God? Why is it not optional, but a must for every child of God? Do you even know that you might be doing it indirectly already? These and many more will be explored extensively in this book.

This book will give insight into the following:

- *Meaning of Evangelism:* This is very crucial. Because oftentimes, it is easy to say evangelism is for the evangelists, this is not completely true.
- *The Office of an Evangelist:* How does this office differ from all Christians?
- *Importance of Evangelism:* Many might wonder what is in evangelism for them? Remember, the Bible says in

1 Timothy 5:18b NLT, "those who work deserve their pay." Every command of God, command blessings.

- *Types of Evangelism:* God creates and loves diversity. He made us in different colors, shapes and He is interested in moving us from glory to glory (See Proverbs 4:18). In the same way, there is a chance, you and I may do evangelism differently.
- *Hurdles and how to overcome:* For every command of God expect resistance. But understanding the power we possess and how to overcome is crucial.
- *Holiness vs. Legalism.*
- *Fear vs. Love and many more.*

May God bless you as you read in Jesus' name. Amen.

About the Author

Ebenezer Agboola is a teacher in the body of Christ. The core of his call is to "bring the light of understanding into the darkness of deception by teaching the word of God." He believes that ignorance is a bondage and understanding is freedom. The source of all understanding is the Holy Spirit (2 Corinthians 3:17). Hence his passion to see people seek understanding and apply it properly (wisdom). This nature of his call makes him relevant not just to Christians, but to everyone.

He is the founder of a teaching ministry called *The Ministry of Light international (MOLI)*. The ministry organizes conferences and teaching events as led by the Holy Spirit; where Ebenezer serves as the host minister.

Ebenezer is happily married to Tumininu; and together they are building a family centered on pleasing and thoroughly obeying God.

www.ingramcontent.com/pod-product-compliance
Lightning Source LLC
Chambersburg PA
CBHW070924080526
44589CB00013B/1423